CU00732559

The facts and names in this
in the public domain. Ma
reports are taken from polic. ....
and statements from those involved,
the internet and other reference works
and biographies. Over time some of
the occurrences may have been
exaggerated or embellished. Any parts
of the book not verified by being in
the public record must be treated as
allegations.

ISBN 9781916163348

Updated and re-edited April 2021

AUTHOR'S NOTE   Please read first

Because of the structure of the London criminal population in the period covered by this book, with members flitting between gangs and forming partnerships, falling out and moving on to other combinations, some of the happenings will be relevant and listed in more than one section. In the early days this happened a lot. I have tried to keep this to a minimum but some of the 'geezers' time lines and 'businesses' overlap and to keep continuity some of the happenings need to be mentioned in more than one section. I have kept the names of those involved in the crimes down to the main players, obviously there are others, drivers, fences, lookouts and facilitators but although important in their own way their inclusion would slow down the narrative without adding any important facts.

The likes of the 'geezers' and heists in the book are unlikely to be matched in future as the old style *'pavement artist'* criminal, that is the bank, post office or security van robber met his match with the coming of CCTV, DNA and now car number plate and facial recognition computer programs. The future of robbery is in the internet hacking and cyber ransom business and the use and sale of stolen personal data and other computer files that list peoples' bank account numbers and card details. Violent crime is now nearly always associated with drug dealing and people trafficking and more often than not controlled by European gangs with Albania and Romania being their most likely bases. The archetypal British robber with a jemmy and a balaclava caught in the light of a policeman's torch putting down his swag bag, raising his hands and saying 'It's a fair cop governor' is no more – if it ever was? Enjoy the book and remember if it hasn't been proved in a court of law it must be seen as an allegation.

CHAPTER	TITLE

CHAPTER 1.

1930s THE MESSINA BROTHERS

These five brothers were instrumental in the start of human trafficking and the explosion of prostitution in London in the 1930s. The father of the five Maltese Messina brothers was Giuseppe Messina from Linguaglossa in Sicily, a Mafia soldier. In late 1890 he came to Malta and worked in a brothel in the notorious Strait Street (Triq Strada Stretta) in Valletta. He married a Maltese woman from Zejtun with the surname De Bono and had two sons Salvatore (born 20 August 1898), and Alfredo (born 6 February 1901). He then moved to Alexandria in Egypt in 1905 where there was a thriving Maltese community and built up a chain of brothels. The other three sons were Eugenio born 1908 in Alexandria, Egypt, Attillo born 1910 in Alexandria and Carmelo born 1915 in Egypt. All the five brothers joined their father in running brothels and prostitution. In 1932 the Egyptian authorities expelled Giuseppe and his sons. The family returned to Malta as Giuseppe had Maltese citizenship from his marriage. In 1934 Eugenio the third son of Giuseppe, moved to London with his French prostitute wife Colette. She helped establish the sex trade in London. The other Messina brothers followed Eugenio and established themselves in Soho soon after.

On arriving in UK the Messina brothers took up English names. Eugenio became Edward Marshal, Carmelo became Charles Maitland, Alfredo became Alfred Martin, Salvatore became Arthur Evans and Atillio became Raymond Maynard. Cheap properties were bought up throughout the West End and Soho and brothels set up. During the years following the Second World War the brothers brought in women from Belgium, France and Spain. With a steady and highly profitable prostitution operation and adequate protection from bribed members of the Metropolitan Police Vice Squad, the Messinas hold on prostitution and trafficking ran unchecked in the city. By the late 1940s they were operating thirty brothels on Queen Street, Bond Street and Stafford Street. The women handed over 80 per cent of their earnings to the brothers for premises and protection. By the 1950s the police estimated that at least 200 of London's most glamorous and expensive prostitutes were Messina girls. Prosecution proved difficult as many of the women who worked for them had valid UK passports, making it hard to make a case for deportation of either the women or the brothers.

Later they started recruiting local English girls by the age old technique of giving good looking girls a good time and promises of marriage followed by being inducted into prostitution.

Attilio Messina reportedly told the press, 'We Messinas are more powerful than the British Government. We do as we like in England.' Which had an element of truth in it as they had most of the Vice Squad taking bribes and a few MPs and Government Officials visiting their girls quite regularly for free and then often being shown photos taken through one way mirrors of those visits when the Social Services started poking around and asking questions of the girls.

An intrepid crime reporter called Duncan Webb who worked for the People Newspaper in the late 1940s started writing articles on the involvement of senior CID officers with the Messinas and published a front page banner headline article on 3rd September 1950 'Arrest these Four Men' Why he said four when there were five active brothers is not known. The articles described the brothers business in the West End and contained interviews with prostitutes revealing names, dates plus photographs and other information that could be the basis for a police investigation. This gained the attention of senior Home Office officials who put together a task force under Superintendent Guy Mahon to go after them. By the end of the 1950's things were getting pretty hot for the Messinas who were tipped off that arrests were imminent. All except Alfredo fled the country on 19th March 1951. Alfredo was arrested and charged with living off immoral earnings and attempting to bribe Superintendent Mahon who was the arresting officer. He was sent down for two years and later joined by Attilio who was caught trying to re-enter the country illegally and sentenced on the same charges to four years. On their release they went to live in Italy setting up brothels and procuring girls from Belgium for the Italian Mafia. Eugenio and Carmelo were arrested in Brussels in 1955 as they were closing a prostitution deal with Belgian girls. They were charged with procuring women, illegal possession of firearms, having fake passports and entering Belgium illegally. Euginio got six years and amazingly Carmelo was acquitted through lack of evidence although the police forces of Britain, Italy, Belgium and France were all involved in submitting evidence. Carmelo was later arrested in1958 for illegal immigration when found asleep in a car in Knightsbridge. He got six months and was then deported to San Remo, Italy where he probably joined his brother Attilio. The Messinas were getting older and younger criminals were moving into the lucrative prostitution rackets as they faded from the picture to live out the rest of their lives in Italy, Belgium or Malta where they had associates.

****

CHAPTER 2.

1940s-70s BERNIE SILVER

Bernard "Bernie" Silver (December 1922, Hackney London – 2002, Westminster London) was an English criminal who was a leading crime boss in the London underworld of the 1950s to 1970s. Active in prostitution, pornography and racketeering, Silver was described as 'a working-class East Ender with a taste for fine restaurants and flashy clothes.'

Silver was born into a Jewish family to Emily V (née Saunders) and Louis Silver, and had three younger brothers, Raymond, Dennis and Ronald.

Silver's rise to prominence began in the mid 1950s with the absorption of the remnants of the Messina Brothers prostitution operation into what came to be known as 'The Syndicate', a criminal organisation headed principally by Silver and a former Maltese traffic policeman 'Big Frank' Mifsud who worked in olive oil importation when he first came to London before becoming part of the Messina gang. In 1956, Silver was arrested and charged for living off immoral earnings but was inexplicably let off by the judge who decided there was no case to answer, (judicial bribery was rife at the time). Starting off with just one strip club in Bower Street, by the late 60's the duo of Silver and Mifsud controlled 19 of the 24 strip clubs in Soho and nearly all of the prostitutes.

During the heyday of their Syndicate (1967–1972), most of the Metropolitan Police Obscene Publications Squad were in their pay, including the squad's head, Detective Chief Superintendent Bill Moody.

Silver's influence began to wane as the 1970s wore on, a decline prompted by major investigations into police corruption that by the end of 1972 had led to the resignation of eighty London detectives. The discovery of a detailed ledger of the Syndicate's police payoffs during a raid on the home of a Silver associate Jimmy Humphreys led to the dismissal or forced retirement of hundreds of Metropolitan Police officers. Corruption trials in 1976–77 resulted in thirteen detectives—including two ex-commanders, the highest-ranking British police officers ever to be convicted of corruption, being sentenced to a total of 90 years in prison.

In 1973, Silver was again arrested and charged with living off immoral earnings for renting out a room above one of their strip clubs to dancers who also worked as prostitutes. He was sentenced to 6 years in prison. Mifsud went on the run before getting caught in Switzerland and deported back to England. However, he appealed and got his sentenced quashed and he then returned to his native Malta.

Silver was also convicted on 8th July 1975 of the murder of Tommy 'Scarface' Smithson (see section later) on 25th June 1956. He was sentenced to life imprisonment for the murder and to ten years imprisonment for conspiracy to murder, but later cleared on appeal. Smithson was a former boxer and merchant navy stoker who had been attempting to take over control of prostitution in Soho.

The film character Lew Vogel in the film The Bank Job is based on Bernie Silver.

Silver's later activities remain unreported and he died in 2002.

****

CHAPTER 3

1950-80s BIG FRANK MIFSUD

The one-time traffic policeman had left Malta in the 1950s to make a name for himself in the vice world of London's Soho where his 18 stone build would ultimately earn him the nick name that hinted at a violent temper, 'Big Frank' Mifsud. He recruited Maltese criminals to the Soho gang that would become known as 'The Syndicate', a vast call-girl empire built up in London over 20 years with Bernie Silver.

The foundations of the gang were laid by a family of Sicilians who at one time lived in Malta, the Messina brothers who we mention earlier, who followed in their father's footsteps as brothel-keepers.

When Scotland Yard swept the Messina gang away in the 1950s, the foundations for other gangsters to take over were laid.

Bernie Silver, born in 1922 into a Jewish family from the East End, joined forces with former traffic policeman Frank Mifsud and they began their rise to prominence starting in the 1950s by taking over what was left of the Italian Messina Brothers empire. (see section on Silver)

The prostitutes operating from their premises in Soho and Mayfair earned between £200 and £500 a week. The Syndicate acquired property in Soho, running strip clubs in the basement or ground floors whilst in the floors above, prostitutes operated full-time in separate flats for which they paid £100-a-week minimum rent.

In the vice crime trial of the Bernie Silver gang of 1974, the Maltese Syndicate met its demise. Silver and nine men, mostly Maltese, were charged with living off immoral earnings between 1955 and 1973.

Frank Mifsud fled when the gang was rounded up, but was detained in Switzerland and held in custody there before being sent back to the UK for trial.

'These men indeed have made a rich living,' prosecutor Michael Corkery said at the trial. Documents found in Silver's Knightsbridge flat revealed ownership of a twin-diesel yacht, credit facilities in a Belgian bank, and property interests in the Channel Islands. 'That's just the tip of the iceberg,' Corkery told the court, saying the Syndicate acted as rent collectors from some 30 Soho prostitution houses.

The Met police said the Syndicate would collect over £100,000 in rents from prostitutes every week.

Mifsud and Silver never dealt directly with girls, leaving the collection to their front-men who collected the cash, deducted their own fees, then passed the remainder on to the bosses. 'So the Syndicate prospered with the main characters keeping well into the background all the time. They hid behind the others successfully for many years until the day of reckoning came,' the prosecutor had said.

A series of trials and exposes revealed a general picture of police-criminal links. Particularly favored were Silver and Mifsud, with the discovery of a detailed ledger of the Syndicate's police payoffs during a raid on the home of Silver associate Jimmy Humphreys. (see Bernie Silver section)

One of the men who collected takings from the prostitutes was Big   Frank's own brother Joseph Mifsud who acted in a managerial role and was also a shareholder. From time to time, in his brother's absence, he also received the money collected from the girls.

Two other Syndicate members Victor 'Bajzu' Micallef and Fred Brett faced charges of kidnapping another Maltese associate, Frank Dyer, who they suspected of having shopped the crime ring to the police.

Dyer originally had come to London in 1947 where he married a Soho prostitute and collected rent for the Syndicate. He was twice jailed for living off her immoral earnings and left the country for Malta in 1959 after a warrant was issued for his arrest for again living off immoral earnings. Dyer later returned in August 1973 to discuss the purchase of a Berwick Street property in Soho as the crime ring started selling off the properties after the News of the World exposed the extent of the business and its ties with the police. But when the Syndicate suspected Dyer of having given the police a statement, they kidnapped him from a London pub, beat him up in a basement cellar and threatened him with a gun, and then offered him £20,000 to disappear so as not to turn up as a witness at the trial of the Syndicate. Which he accepted and failed to turn up.

Silver would be sentenced to six years in prison before Mifsud got extradited from Switzerland to face the same charges. But he would later get his sentence quashed on appeal.

In the UK, Big Frank was also tried and cleared of the 1956 murder of gangster Thomas 'Scarface' Smithson, 36, having denied ordering the killing of the protection racketeer. Silver was convicted on 8 July, 1975 of the murder, sentenced to life imprisonment for murder and to ten years' imprisonment for conspiracy to murder, but later cleared on appeal. Mifsud's trial followed information on the murder given to police in the 1973 bust.

Mifsud had a share in a gambling club run by Maltese national George Caruana, who, however, had to pay Smithson protection money – five shillings in the pound. Caruana later closed the club and moved to the East End, but Smithson would not let him go. On the first occasion when he went to collect the money, Smithson arrived with ten men armed with iron bars, and Caruana paid up.

Vince Farrugia, a Maltese national who also ran a gambling club in the East End, heard Mifsud say of Smithson: 'We will have to get rid of him.' It was alleged he hired underworld gunman Philip Ellul, also a Maltese, to kill Smithson. Ellul had been charged along with Victor Spampinato in 1956 for the murder of Smithson, by shooting him with a revolver in a Maida Vale boarding house. Ellul claimed Smithson had threatened to kill him. On the evening of 25 June, 1956, he and Spampinato went to see George Caruana at 'Blondie Bate's' boarding house, where he found Smithson inside. 'While talking to Miss Bates I saw her looking at something, and turning around, I saw Smithson with a pair of scissors in his hand,' Ellul told the court. 'He said, 'I am going to have you now' and made a swing at me and I pulled out the gun. I ducked and hit him on the chin with my fist and he fell on the bed, He jumped up in no time and was after me. I thought he was going to stab me so I shot him.'

The prosecution, however, said Smithson had gone to the boarding house for a business meeting with the landlord, and that while he waited in a flat, Ellul came in and shot him in the neck.

That same prosecution alleged Mifsud helped organise Smithson's killing, and that shortly before a remand appearance in 1975 at a London court, Mifsud said of Smithson, 'He was a blackmailer. He only got what he deserved he was always making me look small. I'm sorry, but he deserved it.'

Ellul was sentenced to death but reprieved four days before execution. He served 11 years of a life sentence and then went to America. In 1974 he was found destitute at age 47 on a park bench in San Francisco, and he voluntarily came back to the UK as chief witness in the case against Bernie Silver and Frank Mifsud. But he changed his mind, probably after being threatened, and returned to the USA. The jury of six men and six women took more than eight hours to bring in a verdict at the end of the week-long trial.

Carmelo Sultana, a Maltese cook, was however jailed in June 1976 for five nights after being found guilty of plotting with others to pervert justice over inquiries into the murder of Smithson. Sultana, then aged 45, denied conspiring with others to bribe the jurors and Ellul.

Frank Mifsud was also found guilty and jailed for five years and fined £50,000 for bribing Harold Stocker to commit perjury during a criminal court trial of Maltese gangsters Anthony Cauchi and Tony Galea. The offence was the result of three petrol bomb explosions at the clubs at the end of 1966 and the beginning of 1967, allegedly at the behest of Mifsud. Cauchi was jailed for five years and Galea for two years. Harold Stocker, who ran a hotdog stall in Soho, had given false evidence in the trial of the two men.

Frank's brother Joe was later jailed for two years along with Joseph Fenech and Emmaneul Borg, for trying to bribe Stocker not to appear as a witness.

Big Frank was until the last minute convinced he would avoid prison time. Witness Dr George Grant, senior medical officer at Brixton Prison, was scolded by Judge McKinnon for attempting to have Mifsud remanded into a mental institution without any prison sentence. The judge said 'This seems to indicate a lack of touch with reality, for a senior medical officer because Mifsud could be free from a mental hospital inside 12 months.' Opinion has it that Grant had been bribed which is why Big Frank thought he would not go to prison.

****

CHAPTER 4

1950s TOMMY 'SCARFACE' SMITHSON

After the War, the vice and gambling industries in Soho were run by gangs as we have seen in the earlier chapters. The main ones were the Maltese Messina Brothers, and the London born Billy Hill and Jack Spot. They controlled their interests by bribing the police and with the threat of a razor attack for anyone who stepped out of line. As one gang member coldly put it, 'People were paid a pound a stitch, so if you put twenty stitches in a man you got a score. You used to look in the papers next day to see how much you'd earned.'

One person who dared to defy the gangs was Tommy Smithson. Born in Liverpool in 1920, the sixth of eight children, his family moved to the East End of London two years later. Tommy served time for theft in a reform school where he learned self-defence and boxing. During the War he joined the merchant navy as a stoker and served on ammunition ships sailing to Australia. He returned to Shoreditch, London in 1950 and was soon sentenced to 18 months for a robbery. In prison he got to know people who ran the Soho gambling clubs and by 1954 he had his own gang which included the young Kray twins, Ronnie and Reggie, who looked up to Smithson as a hero and mentor. The Maltese gang members had taken advantage of subsidised passages to England for as little as three pounds and had established a network of gambling and drinking clubs servicing a string of prostitutes they brought to the UK by the same subsidised passage cost. Smithson decided to target those Maltese. He began by working as a croupier for George Caruana in one of his clubs in Batty Street, Stepney. Caruana and his Maltese colleagues were keen to avoid trouble and when Smithson set up a protection racket he was soon taking a regular share of the takings in all their 'spielers'. The club owners paid him a shilling in the pound, it doesn't sound much but Tommy was making up to £500 a night. He opened his own clubs, such as the Publishers Club, supposedly for authors – but nobody was fooled! Then following police raids, he went to Brixton prison until a whip round of his friends paid the heavy fine. He started to seriously annoy people when he set up as a bookmaker in Berwick Street, in competition with Billy Hill and Jack Spot.

He got into a fight and cut Freddie 'Slip' Sullivan in French Henry's club with a flick knife. Sullivan had a brother in the Hill-Spot gang and retribution was swift. Smithson was told a peace offering was on the table and that there was no reason the gangs couldn't get along together. He went to meet Spot and Hill behind the Carreras 'Black Cat' cigarette factory in Camden Town. He was carrying a gun, but surprisingly handed it over when asked to by Billy Hill. The signal for the attack on Tommy was a cigar butt being thrown down and ground out. He was slashed in the face, arms, legs and body and then thrown over a wall into Regents Park near Park Village East, to bleed to death. Amazingly he survived and 47 stitches were put into his face. As a reward for honoring the 'code of silence' he was paid £500 from Billy Hill and earned his nickname of 'Scarface'. Tommy opened more clubs and fenced stolen goods for a time but he got another set of stitches when the word spread that he was a 'grass'. This ended his entry into the big time and he decided it was safer to work as a protector for the Maltese. Tommy fell in love with Fay Richardson, a mill girl from Stockport who came to London to work as a prostitute in the Maltese clubs. The press described her as a 'gangster's moll' and a 'femme fatale'. She was certainly dangerous to know as three of her lovers were murdered and others suffered severe beatings. In his memoirs Commander Bert Wickstead of Scotland Yard said, 'She couldn't have been described as a beautiful woman by any stretch of the imagination. Yet she did have the most devastating effect on the men in her life, so there must have been something about the lady.' The handsome and dapper Smithson and his money appealed to Fay and they began living together. When she was held on remand for bouncing cheques Tommy raised money for her defence. He collected £50 from his former employer, George Caruana, but complained bitterly that it should have been a £100. On 13 June 1956 Smithson and two other men confronted Caruana and fellow Maltese Philip Ellul who ran a small prostitute racket and asked for more money. In the ensuing fight Caruana was cut on the fingers as he protected his face. Another £30 was produced at gunpoint and in line with standard gangland practice, Ellul was ordered to start a collection book for Fay's defence. But Tommy had gone too far this time, just two weeks later on 25 June 1956, he was found dying in a Kilburn gutter outside number 88 Carlton Vale near the junction with Cambridge Road, the house was a brothel owned by Caruana. Smithson thought he'd been sent there to collect protection money. He was in the room of 'Blonde Mary' Bates when Philip Ellul, Vic

Spampinato and Joe Zammit came in. Ellul shot him in the arm and the neck but the .38 revolver jammed and Smithson ran off crawling down the stairs into the street. Bizarrely, his last words to the people who found him were said to be, 'Good morning, I'm dying.' He was taken to Paddington Hospital but died shortly after he arrived.

The hit men, who fled to America, were reassured they'd only be charged with manslaughter if they turned themselves in. But it was a police ploy and they were tried for murder when they returned to the UK. Spampinato told the court he was only defending himself when Smithson attacked him with a pair of scissors. 'Blonde Mary' confirmed the story and he was acquitted. But it later emerged that Blonde Mary was Spampinato's girlfriend. Ellul was sentenced to death for murder. Then 48 hours before his execution, the sentence was commuted to life when the police offer of a manslaughter charge only that had been made to get him back to the UK became public knowledge, he served eleven years in prison. After he was released Ellul came to London to collect the money had been promised by the organization. Sixpence was thrown on the floor and he was ordered to pick it up and then he was taken to Heathrow for a flight to America and warned, 'Don't ever come back. If you do we have a pair of concrete boots waiting for you'. He did as he was told and stayed in America.

Smithson's funeral was an old style gangster one, Rolls Royce hearses, elaborate floral tributes and members of 'the firm' attending. Thousands watched as the coffin was taken to St Patrick's Cemetery in Leytonstone. The young Kray twins were there but Fay was still under arrest and wasn't allowed to attend the funeral. She sent a wreath saying, 'Till we meet again, Love Fay'. She was put on probation that August and ordered to live with her mother in Stockport. Later, Smithson's dear old mum who was well respected in the East End, had a large statue of an angel put on the grave. One of the Kray firm said, 'I had to laugh, a villain like Tommy Smithson with an angel over his grave!' As crime reporter Duncan Campbell graphically says in his book, 'The Underworld', 'There were almost as many theories as to why Smithson had died as there were scars in his face'. The background behind Tommy's killing didn't become clear until 17 years later. In October 1973 'The Old Grey Fox' Bert Wickstead, one of the

Big Five at Scotland Yard, was leading the Serious Crime Squad. He decided to move against the Syndicate who had taken over most of the vice in Soho after the Messina brothers had been deported. They were said to be earning as much as £100,000 a week, the organisation was run by Bernie Silver (the only non-Maltese member), and 18 stone Big Frank Mifsud.

Just as the police raids were due, Silver and Mifsud had taken off on an 'extended holiday' after being tipped off by a member of Wickstead's team. So Wickstead went through an elaborate pretence of having the warrants withdrawn and leaked a story to the press that he had given up the case. The papers responded with stories along the lines of, 'The Raid That Never Was'. The ruse worked and members of the Syndicate started to return to London. Bernie Silver was arrested while he was having dinner with his girlfriend at the Park Tower Hotel on 30 December 1973.

Other members of the gang were seized at the Scheherazade Club in Soho. In the early hours of the morning Wickstead had stepped on stage to announce that everyone was arrested. One person shouted out, 'What do you think of the cabaret?' and another wit replied, 'Not much!' The guests, staff and even the band, were taken to Limehouse police station where the band continued playing and everyone sang songs. A total of 170 members of the Syndicate were taken into custody but Frank Mifsud had been warned about the raid and had fled abroad.

Wickstead said that Silver and Mifsud had ordered the murder of Tommy Smithson. The argument was that when Smithson had demanded money for Fay Richardson's defence and an increase in his protection rate, it came at a bad time for Silver who was preparing to expand his empire. He couldn't afford to be seen as a weak man by giving in to a small time crook like Smithson, so he told Ellul and Spampinato to get rid of him. Wickstead and his team traced Spampinato to Malta. Elluh was run to ground in San Francisco after 'The Old Grey Fox' had appeared on an American TV show and a photo of Elluh appeared in the magazine, 'True Detective'. Both men agreed to return to London and testify against the Syndicate in return for police protection.

Spampinato gave useful evidence at the committal proceedings but refused to attend the Old Bailey trial. Elluh did not give any evidence in court. He managed to slip away from the police who were protecting him and returned to America. The grapevine said the price of their silence was at least £35,000 apiece.

Frank Mifsud was extradited from a Swiss clinic after claiming he was mentally unfit to stand trial. In December 1974 after a long trial, he and Bernie Silver were given six years for living off immoral earnings. Then in July 1975 Silver was sentenced to life imprisonment for Smithson's murder but a year later the Court of Appeal squashed the conviction, as they said that the case had been built on the evidence of unreliable witnesses. In 1976 Mifsud was also tried at the Old Bailey for ordering Smithson's killing. He said he was a property and club owner earning £50,000 a year. He claimed that he was a friend of Smithson and was very sorry to hear he had been killed. When asked if he knew that Billy Hill had occasionally employed Smithson as a gangster Mifsud simply said that Billy Hill was, 'a kind gentleman who lent money'. Mifsud was acquitted of the murder but sentenced to five years imprisonment for living off immoral earnings. This was overturned by the Court of Appeal the following year.

Friends close to Smithson always maintained that the Maltese had become tired of paying him off and organized his killing. One said the message to British gangsters was, 'Watch out for the "Epsom Salts" (Malts), they will retaliate.' But according to Philip Elluh, the motive was far more mundane. After Smithson had attacked him and George Caruana, Elluh heard that Tommy was going to shoot him. So he went looking for him, and when he found Tommy in Carlton Vale he simply shot him first.

****

CHAPTER 5
1930s-60s BILLY HILL

Billy Hill was a mentor to the Krays and one of the most influential gangsters in the UK of all time. The value of his heists would put him far ahead of most of the current ones if converted into today's money equivalent. William 'Billy' Charles Hill (13 December 1911 – 1 January 1984) was an English criminal, linked to smuggling, protection rackets, and extreme violence. He was one of the foremost perpetrators of organised crime in London from the 1920s through to the 1960s and head of the Camden Hill Mob in the 50's. He project managed cash robberies and, in a clever scam, defrauded London's High Society of millions at the card tables of John Aspinall's Clermont Club.

Hill was born in Fitzrovia, Central London to Frances Mary A Hill (née Sparling) and Frederick Joseph Hill, who married in 1888.

Growing up in an established criminal family Hill committed his first stabbing at age fourteen. He began as a house burglar in the late 1920s and then specialized in 'smash-and-grab' raids targeting furriers and jewelers in the 1930s. During World War II, Hill moved into the black market, specializing in foods and petrol. He also supplied forged documents for deserting servicemen and was involved in West End protection rackets with fellow gangster Jack Spot (they later fell out) and tied in with the Messina Brothers as 'minders' to some of the Messina's 'girls'. In the late 1940s, he was charged with burgling a warehouse and fled to South Africa. Following an arrest there for assault, he was extradited back to Britain where he was convicted for the warehouse robbery and served time in prison. This was his last jail term. After his release he met Gypsy Riley, better known as 'Gypsy Hill', who became his common-law wife. In 1952 he planned the Eastcastle Street postal van robbery (see chapter 6) netting £287,000 (2021 value £11.5 million), and in 1954 he organised a £40,000 bullion heist. No one was ever convicted for these robberies. He also ran drug, cigarette and wine smuggling operations from Morocco during this period.

In 1955, Hill wrote his memoir Boss of Britain's Underworld. In it he described his use of the shiv (knife) 'I was always careful to draw my knife down on the face, never across or upwards. Always down. So that if the knife slips you don't cut an artery. After all, chivving is chivving, but cutting an artery is usually murder. Only mugs do murder.'

Hill was mentor to twins Ronnie and Reggie Kray, advising them in their early criminal careers.

In late 1956 Home Secretary Gwilym Lloyd George authorized the tapping of Hill's phone. At the time gang warfare had broken out in London between Hill and erstwhile partner in crime, Jack 'Spot' Comer. In 1956, Spot and wife Rita were attacked by Hill's bodyguard, Frankie Fraser plus Bobby Warren and at least half a dozen other men. Both Fraser and Warren were given seven years for their acts of violence.

The Bar Council approached the police and requested the tapes in order to provide evidence for an investigation into the professional conduct of Hill's barrister, Patrick Marrinan. Sir Frank Newsam, Permanent Secretary at the Home Office, allowed them access. When this use of tapping powers was revealed to Parliament in June 1957, Leader of the Opposition Hugh Gaitskell demanded a full explanation. Rab Butler pledged that it would not be a precedent and that he would consider withdrawing the evidence and asking the Bar council to disregard it. Marrinan was subsequently disbarred and expelled by Lincoln's Inn, but Butler was forced to appoint a committee of Privy Counsellors under Sir Norman Birkett to look into the prerogative power of intercepting telephone communications.

In the 1960s Hill was busy fleecing aristocrats at gaming club card tables. This was before the Gaming Club Rules were brought into law by Sir Stanley Raymond and it was a free for all with no limits set on any gambling and no suitability checks on anybody asking for a license to run a club. Hence the number of small gaming clubs set up by the Krays and the Richardsons in London. Hill was a partner in crime with John Aspinall at his Clermont Club in London's West End. In Douglas Thompson's book The Hustlers, and the subsequent documentary on Channel 4, The Real Casino Royale, the club's former financial director John Burke and Hill's associate Bobby McKew, claimed that John Aspinall (one of Lord Lucan's best friends and alleged to have been involved in Lucan's disappearance) worked with Hill to cheat the players at the Clermont Club. Some of the wealthiest people in Britain were swindled out of millions of pounds, thanks to a gambling con known as "the Big Edge".

Marked cards could be discovered too easily as could

phosphor lined ones so instead the low cards were slightly bent across their width in a small mangle before being repackaged. High cards were slightly bent lengthwise. Hill's men were trained to distinguish the bends and were introduced to the tables by Aspinall where they could read whether a card was high, low or an unbent zero card (10 to king) thus gaining a 60-40 *edge*. The final stage involved 'skimming' the profits from the tables to avoid attention. On the first night of the *edge* operation, the tax-free winnings for the house were £14,000 (2021 value £880,000). According to McKew, the 18th Earl of Derby lost £40,000 (2021 value £1.8 million) in one night.

The club's former financial director John Burke quit in late 1965, a year into the scam. He had been tipped off about an undercover police investigation but Aspinall was determined to carry on. However, Aspinall no longer had someone to deal with 'the dirty end' of the operation, paying the criminals at the tables and laundering the money. After two years operation Aspinall got jittery and the Big Edge was closed. Hill respected Aspinall's decision, and the partnership dissolved.

Hill was also involved in property development. He bought the biggest nightclub in Tangier, Churchills, for Gypsy which she ran from 1966 until the mid-1970s where it is alleged the biggest money laundering business in Europe went on with much of the money from the big UK heists being 'washed' there. Hill retired from crime in the 1970s and died on 1 January 1984, aged 72.

In 1963, Mickey Spillane was playing Mike Hammer in The Girl Hunters filming in London where he met Hill and showed him around the set. When the prop department couldn't find Spillane a real M1911 pistol, Hill brought the producers several real ones the next day to use in the film.

****

CHAPTER 6

1952 EASTCASTLE STREET ROBBERY

The Eastcastle Street robbery was, at the time, Britain's largest post-war robbery. It occurred on Wednesday 21st May 1952 in Eastcastle Street when seven masked men held up a post office van just off Oxford Street, central London. The robbery was helped by Oxford Street being closed for road works and the Eastcastle Street diversion being much narrower and less busy. The robbers escaped with £287,000 estimated to be worth £11.5m in 2020.

The robbers used two cars to sandwich the post office van. The first car emerged slowly from a side street causing the van to slow down, the second car then pulled up alongside. The driver and two attendants were dragged out, coshed and the van was stolen. It was later found abandoned near Regents Park, 18 of the 31 mailbags were missing. Investigators found that the van's alarm bell had been tampered with prior to the hold up which meant an insider with overnight access to the van must have been involved. The insider theory was underlined by the gang knowing that such an abnormally large amount of cash would be in this particular van on that particular day. It was not just coincidence.

The robbery heralded the start of so called 'project managed' crime in the UK, the criminal carefully planning a crime. Rehearsals for the Eastcastle heist had been carried out in the roads outside London under the pretext that a crime movie was being shot. The mastermind behind the raid was London gangster Billy Hill (see previous section) and the robbers included George 'Taters' Chatham and Terry Hogan, well known 'faces' to the police. A £25,000 reward was offered for information leading to recovery of the money and a thousand police officers took part in searches, but the robbers were never caught and no money ever recovered.

Prime Minister Winston Churchill demanded daily updates on the police investigation and the Postmaster General was required to report to Parliament on what had gone wrong.

****

CHAPTER 7
1940s-60s JACK 'SPOT' COMER

Born Jacob Colmore in Mile End , London, Jack 'spot' Comer was the youngest of four children, Comer's father was a Jewish tailor's machinist who had moved to London with his wife from Poland in 1903. In order to integrate into English society, the family changed their name from Comacho to Colmore, and later to Comer. His mother's maiden name was Lifschinska. Jack Comer grew up in a Jewish street in Fieldgate Mansions, Whitechapel, on the west side of Myrdle Street, across from the Irish community in terraced houses along the east side. At the age of seven Jack had joined his first gang which was made up of boys from the Jewish side of Myrdle Street who fought their Catholic rivals from the other end of the street. Comer soon started being called 'spotty' because he had a big black mole on his left cheek and that soon became abbreviated to 'Spot'. 'Spot' Comer was very politically minded and took part in the Battle of Cable Street. He and his mob clashed with police and charged into the fascists with full power, injuring as many 'Blackshirts' and police as possible. "Spot" found himself standing alone when the others fled and was surrounded by police with truncheons. He was badly beaten and sent to hospital and then prison. In the post-war era Comer was involved in funding the 43 Group, a Jewish street gang that clashed with the equally violent supporters of the Union Movement and other more minor far right groups. Comer allegedly financed and masterminded the raid on the BOAC secure warehouse at Heathrow on 28 July 1948 (see chapter 9). The raid was foiled by the Flying Squad in what became known as 'The Battle of Heathrow'. Spot's control of the East End rackets loosened in 1952 when his former partner, gangster Billy Hill, was released from prison after Spot's failed £1.25 million heist on Heathrow Airport. Off-course bookmaking was also about to become legalized at this time, creating another dent in Spot's income. In 1954 Comer attacked crime journalist Duncan Webb of the Sunday People newspaper and was fined £50. He was accused of possession of a knuckle duster and convicted of grievous bodily harm. In 1955 he was arrested following a knife fight with Albert Dimes, (see Dimes section). Spot was cleared of the stabbing charge. In 1956, Spot and his then wife Rita were attacked outside their Paddington home by 'Mad' Frankie Fraser (see Fraser's section) and Bobby Warren on the orders of Billy Hill with whom he had fallen out over money owed to Hill. Both Fraser and Warren were given seven years in prison. Spot retired 'whilst I'm still alive' and progressively withdrew from crime. He did many jobs over the years; barman, fruit seller and antiques dealer, to name a few. His ashes were spread in Israel after he died in 1996.

CHAPTER 8
1940s – 70s BERT 'BATTLES' ROSSI

Bert 'Battles' Rossi died in 2017 at the University College Hospital in North London after falling and breaking two ribs at his home in Islington at the age of 94. The service was held at St Peter's Italian church in Holborn and the crematorium ceremony was bookended by theme music from the films The Godfather and Once Upon a Time in America. He was close friends and adviser to many of the 'names' in the underworld including crime boss Terry Adams, a one time a neighbor, Adams was said to be absent from the funeral due to the presence of the press but sent a wreath to mark his respects.

Roberto Alberto Rossi was an English gangster and former mentor and associate of the Kray twins known as the 'General of Clerkenwell'. He stood trial for murder in 1975 but was acquitted. A journalist linked him to 11 murders, a figure which he did not dispute.

Born in Clerkenwell as Roberto Alberto Rossi in 1922 to Italian immigrants who moved to what is known as 'Little Italy' after World War 1. Rossi lived in Islington all his life, most recently in Colebrooke Row, Angel. Rossi, whose full first name was Roberto, got his nickname because his mother would shout 'Berto!' from the window when he was playing football in the street and with her Italian accent, it sounded to the English boys like "Battles". Since he was constantly fighting, on one occasion splitting open another boy's head because he had mimicked his mother, the name stuck. The boy was later put in hospital for ten days by Rossi, who was prevented from doing more damage by Albert Dimes stepping in and pulling him off. His mother got him a job at the Savoy Hotel in the Strand where he saw the good life and made up his mind to 'get some for myself'.

His father worked as an ice-cream seller but the family always struggled financially. He left school at 14, later describing himself as 'a naughty boy' and began his life of crime by breaking into a butcher's shop and stealing a turkey after his mother told him they had nothing for Christmas dinner. At 18 he entered the world of organised crime after taking on a local gangster and 'cracking his head right open'. He was conscripted during the war but went AWOL and ended up in the black market. His reputation as a violent, hard man who would use a 'chiv' (knife) at the slightest provocation got him noticed by bigger fish in the underworld and he and his team were often paid to 'do someone on their behalf'.

On Thursday the 28th of June 1956, both Bert 'Battles' Rossi and William Patrick Blythe, one of his team, were arrested in Dublin, Ireland in a dramatic police swoop by Scotland Yard Detectives on a saloon bar. Blythe later received a sentence of 5 years and Rossi a sentence of 4 years for the attack on Jack 'Spot' Comer along with 'Mad' Frankie Fraser. The hit was paid for by Billy Hill who had fallen out with Comer. Rossi later moved into dealing in cocaine but would never touch heroin and ran clubs in Soho, working again for gang leader Billy Hill, and with Albert Dimes another Clerkenwell Italian mobster, running gambling and snooker halls. Mr Rossi married Rene, an Englishwoman, now dead, and the couple had two children, Peter, who has also died, and Irene.

In prison he met Ronnie Kray, who he scorned for 'wanting the limelight' but nevertheless mentored. In the 1960s he became close to prominent American gangsters, meeting Philadelphia crime boss Angelo Bruno and Carlo Gambino who ran the powerful Gambino crime family in New York and the mob's accountant Meyer Lansky. He did many jobs for the Mafia, including as their enforcer in London and looked after people they 'owned' who came to London including world heavyweight champion Rocky Marciano and Frank Sinatra. He also ran illegal gambling clubs himself, recounting that Lucian Freud and Francis Bacon were frequent visitors and 'good friends.' Rossi retired after he was acquitted in 1975 of the murder of Beatrice "Biddy" Gold in the basement of the clothing business she ran in Clerkenwell during a raid on the premises, he denied having anything to do with it. He would still do a bit of 'consultancy work' in his retirement. In his later years Rossi, had a relationship with another English woman, Mary and always kept up his trademark dapper appearance, usually wearing a three-piece suit and watch chain. He enjoyed playing cards, seeing old friends around Islington, shopping at Chapel Market, spending time with his family and putting a bet on the racing. He also reportedly ironed his banknotes because he liked to keep everything neat.

****

CHAPTER 9
THE 1948 BOAC WAREHOUSE HEIST DEBACLE

In 1948 Donald Fish was a former Scotland Yard Detective who was now head of the British Overseas Airways Corporation (BOAC) security at the newly opened Heathrow Airport. He was a worried man as he was not at all happy with the BOAC security that he inherited with the job. Bullion, valuables and other high value items were stored in an old corrugated iron warehouse that used to be a hangar. Since the Airport had opened it had become a main 'go to' place for every petty thief and organised crime gang for rich and easy pickings. The area was not under the protection of the Metropolitan Police and had its own private airport police who were having difficulty in keeping control of the increasing number of thefts. Fish had one big problem looming up. A warehouseman called Anthony Walsh had informed him of an approach by an organised crime team who had offered Walsh £500 to help them steal a consignment of gold that was due in from South America. Fish had checked out Walsh's story and found that all the information on the day and time of the gold's arrival was correct. He realised that his meager police force would be no match for an armed team of professional criminals so he contacted his friend Divisional Detective Inspector Roberts of 'T' Division. Roberts soon realised that with the possibility of a major crime gang being involved his resources could not match what was required and he in turn called in Scotland Yard's elite Flying Squad who had been formed for just such an operation as this.   The Flying Squad had been recently separated from C1 Department which had been a conglomeration of different squads including the Murder Squad and now had its own department tag, C8 and a new boss in Detective Superintendent Bill Chapman. Chapman updated the fast response vehicles the squad had and expanded the personnel to 80 officers, added 27 cars, 3 taxis and 4 vans. He put operational control in the hands of his second in command DCI Bob Lee who knew the London 'mob' scene inside out and had a photographic memory for faces and places. Lee knew the criminal who had approached Walsh with a £500 offer was Alfred Roome, known as 'big Alfie' or 'The Ilford Kid' and had a 42 year long criminal record on file. Lee then spent time checking through Roome's associates and past partners in crime to see who might well be in the gang being formed. He concentrated on Edward William Hughes and Billy Hill who carried out a robbery in 1942 and went to prison for 3 years. On release Hill figured again with Sammy Ross, also known as Sammy Joseph and Teddy Machin in a £9000 Manchester robbery in 1947 for which they were not caught. Hill was also wanted for a warehouse robbery that he denied but was so boxed in by police surveillance on him 24 hours a day which his criminal friends didn't like that he surrendered to police and was sentenced to another 3 years which put him out of the picture for the proposed BOAC heist. But Teddy Machin was at liberty and being the 'chiv' man for Jack 'Spot' Comer who was organising the job he would play an important part. In fact the Vauxhall car Walsh had seen being driven off after the £500 offer from Roome and whose number plate he had noted belonged to Jack Comer. Comer and Hill were the two men ruling London's underworld at the time. Hill, as we have said before, was the first underworld boss to organise his raids as and 'project management' them, meticulously planning and rehearsing each one down to the finest detail and even providing 'pensions' to the families of any of his men caught and incarcerated. He was charismatic and also ruthless with liberal use of a razor to the face of anybody stepping out of line whether they were on his or an opponent's side. Jack Comer was the opposite, a hard man running protection rackets in the East End and against bookmakers at racetracks. He dominated his patch by fear. It was very likely that Jack Comer was putting up the money for the BOAC heist in return for a large cut of the profits. This type of financer was known as a 'thieves ponce'. Comer did not have the intelligence or aptitude to organise such a large job and this was left to Hughes, Ross and Roome who ran it past Billy Hill inside prison for any input he might have. The original plan was based on information that bullion worth a quarter of a million was coming into Heathrow via BOAC from South America via Madrid. The source of this information is unknown. But with Hill's mob contacts it is quite possible it came to him originally for a fee or a smaller upfront fee plus a percentage of the take. As the others were checking out the warehouse and sitting in a pub close to the airport in walked Alfred Walsh. Roome knew the face and recognised him as being a fellow POW in a German Prisoner of War camp at Genshagen. The conversation turned to Walsh's resentment towards BOAC who had demoted him from security guard to warehouseman for some minor infringement of duty and Roome took a chance and made the £500 offer if Walsh would lace the coffee of the three security guards in the warehouse with phenobarbitone tablets to knock them out and then open the doors for the gang to get in.

Walsh initially accepted the plan but had second thoughts later and went to Donald Fish with the story in hope that it might lead to his reinstatement in his old job which was higher pay than warehouseman rates.

Walsh followed the CID instructions and met Roome prior to coming on duty at 8pm on the 28th July and was given the phenobarbitone tablets, had he given them to the guards the strength of those particular tablets was sufficient to kill them. An hour later the plane from Madrid landed and the bullion was off loaded into the BOAC strong room at Chiswick for checking and customs clearance. Then it was put into a BOAC bullion van and transferred to the Heathrow warehouse. The gang checked all the movements and were confident all was going to plan. What they didn't know was that the bullion container unloaded from the van into the warehouse was empty. Behind it in the warehouse and hidden around the warehouse were 14 Flying Squad officers backed up outside the premises by more officers disguised as BOAC personnel and yet more inside a nearby lorry. Two miles away Squad cars were positioned on all the exit routes just in case.

The gold had not made it to the warehouse but there was still a quarter of a million pounds worth of other goods and £14,000 of jewelry in its safe. The three guards had been taken out the back way to a hotel and Detective Sergeants Charlie Hewitt, George Draper and John Matthews had taken their place. In a separate office Donald Fish sat with an open line to Scotland Yard communications room. When the gang entered he would say the code word 'Nora' which was the name of one of the Detective's wives. This would put the police on stand-bye as arrests could only be made once the gang had actually handled goods or broken open containers, any arrest before that would not constitute breaking and entering or robbery and a good barrister would argue that the gang were on a boys night out, got lost and just happened to wander into the warehouse and probably get the case dismissed. Just before midnight a regular mobile canteen arrived outside and Walsh went out to get a jug of coffee which he brought back in. This was the normal coffee break and the gang would be watching to see the coffee go inside for the three security officers.

Inside Walsh poured three cups of coffee and tipped them away, the gang maybe had a back-up plan and might have doped the coffee themselves in the mobile canteen just to make sure. Roome had told Walsh the pills would take 20 minutes to act so after fifteen the decoy officers draped themselves across the table feigning unconsciousness with the cups dropped beside it and one put on its side on it. Walsh now slid open the warehouse's giant doors.

The man the gang sent to check all was okay inside was Sidney Cook the driver of the getaway lorry. He stood peering round the interior in his stolen BOAC uniform carrying a car starting handle, just in case. He called to a second gang member who took a look and then as both were satisfied they signaled and 11 members of the gang walked in.

They were dressed in dark clothes, wore gloves and for the first time in a UK robbery had stockings over their faces. In the back office Donald Fish whispered 'Nora' down the phone. Alfred Roome walked up to the three fake guards and Hewitt who was posing as the guard with the keys on his belt took a slap on the face from Roome. He didn't move so satisfied that the drug had worked Roome took his keys and then put adhesive tape over the three officer's mouths and tied them up. Another member produced a bottle of water and washed out the coffee cups as it had been decide this was a good ploy and could be used again in the future. Roome inserted the key into the large safe and the mechanism emitted a loud click which satisfied the requirements of the larceny act and DDI Roberts stepped out of his hiding place as did the other officers and shouted 'We are police officers of the Flying Squad, stay where you are.' At the same time Donald Fish gave the yard the code word 'In the bag'.

Roome realised he had been set up and was looking at several years in prison which he didn't fancy at all so decided to make a fight of it and shouted, 'Get the guns out and let 'em have it lads, shoot the bastards!' There were no guns but an assortment of street weapons and all Hell broke loose. DCI Bob Lee had his scalp split open from a blow with an iron bar from Alfred Roome. The gangster with the water bottle broke it and ground the jagged end into DS Fred

Allen's thigh, Allen cracked him over the head with his truncheon and both fell to the floor, Allen was conscious but grievously wounded, his opponent was out cold. Draper had been untied and he release Charlie Hewitt who hammered into Roome causing serious injuries. DS Donald MacMillan had his nose broken as he defended Hewitt from an assailant behind him with an iron bar, DS Mickey Downes had his hand smashed by one of the gang wielding a pair of wire cutters, Detective Inspector Peter Sinclair had his arm broken. As the fighting spilled outside the rest of the Squad's waiting men piled in and soon 8 of the gang were laid unconscious on the ground.

Not all of them were caught Bertie Saphir and Billy Benstaed got away and Teddy Machin ran off into the darkness and fell into a deep ditch knocking himself out and was overlooked.(later in 1970 he took both barrels of a sawn off shotgun through the window of his Canning Town house.) Franny Daniels, a major thief, ran off and hid beneath a lorry clinging on as it moved off. He was going to drop off when it stopped, which it did at Harlington Police Station where he scarpered unseen.

The robbers were remanded in custody the next day at Uxbridge Magistrates' court except for Roome who was in hospital. The Magistrate had difficulty in separating the bloodstained and beaten robbers from the bloodstained and beaten Flying Squad Officers before him. Jack Comer denied he was involved and said his car was seen by Walsh because he had lent it to some friends that evening. There was no other evidence linking him to the crime but the police paid so much attention to him and his various clubs that most closed and he was a person no gratis to other villains and with his savage beating by Frankie Fraser and others over a debt to Billy Hill he faded from view and died penniless aged 82 in 1995.

The trial took place at the Old Bailey on 17th September. After listening to some fairly unconvincing mitigation the Recorder of London, Sir Gerald Dodson told them: 'One can only describe this as the battle of the BOAC, for that is what it degenerated into – a battle and nothing less.

It is a thing honest people regard with terror and great abhorrence. All of you men set your minds and hands to this enterprise. You were, of course, playing for high stakes as there was nearly £14,000 worth of jewelry in the safe alone and thousands of pounds' worth of other goods.

You went there with a van to carry it away in and you went armed. It is a little difficult for me under those circumstances to accept the suggestion that the plan here did not involve violence. If that were so, why carry these weapons? If the drug had been successful no violence would be done, but if the drugging were not successful a different set of circumstances would arise. You made sure of your position by being ready for any situation with weapons of all kinds. This is the gravity of the offence. It does not matter that the actual property was some keys. Of course, that is what you were after first of all, the keys. They were the keys to the situation and to the safe. A raid on this scale profoundly shocks society. You went prepared for violence and you got it. You got the worst of it and you can hardly complain about that.' Telling Edward Hughes (the possessor of the weak heart) 'Corporal punishment is not now envisaged by the law, and so, strictly logically, the injuries you have received are no punishment at all – merely part of the risk you ran.' The Recorder imposed the heaviest sentence; twelve years' penal servitude.

As women collapsed and became hysterical in the corridor, Hughes replied, 'Thank you for British Justice.' Sammy Ross was sentenced to eleven years' penal servitude and two brothers, Jimmy and George Wood (the latter was also known as John Wallis) received nine and eight years, respectively. George Smith and Sidney Cook were each sentenced to eight years' penal servitude and William Henry Ainsworth, to five. And what of the hard man Alfred Roome, 'Big Alfie' who had recruited Anthony Walsh and who had been responsible for the savage assault on DCI Bob Lee? As the Recorder sentenced him to ten years' penal servitude, Roome broke down, sank to his knees and sobbed. It was an act which was to have a profound, far-reaching effect. For such a display, Sammy Ross, the gang's leader, ordered that Roome be ostracized in prison. Upon his release his former associates continued this exclusion and after his wife started an affair with a younger man Roome became so unbalanced that he blamed the pair for everything and launched a frenzied attack on them and then took poison. They survived – Roome did not.

Anthony Walsh, who positively identified four of the gang to the

Flying Squad, was dealt with at a separate hearing; he was bound over to be of good behavior for a period of two years.

****

CHAPTER 10

1960s-70s BERTIE SMALLS 'SUPERGRASS'

Derek Creighton "Bertie" Smalls (1935 – January 31, 2008) was considered by many as Britain's first SUPERGRASS. Although there have been informers throughout history, the Kray Twins were partly convicted two years before Smalls on evidence given by Leslie Payne but the Smalls case was significant for three reasons, firstly he was the first informer to give the police a book of the names of his associates and provide the evidence that would send dozens of them to prison to serve long sentences, secondly he was the first criminal informer to make a written, legally binding deal with the Director of Public Prosecutions; and thirdly he was the only criminal informer to serve no time for his crime in return for providing Queen's Evidence

In 1972, Sir Robert Mark became Commissioner of the Metropolitan Police. That year, the annual total of armed robberies in the Metropolitan Police district was 380, partly because the culture was rife with bribe-taking, sharing in the proceeds of crime and "verballing", or fabricating evidence against suspects. Sir Robert felt compelled to remind his detectives which side of the law they were supposed to be on, he told them in his inaugural address a line that became famous in law keeping circles, 'A good police force is one that catches more criminals than it employs.'

At the centre of Sir Robert's focus was the CID, and at its rotten pinnacle was the Flying Squad. Ken Drury, commander of the Flying Squad and one of his inspectors, Alistair Ingram, later went to prison for corruption. They weren't the only ones. Sir Robert delegated the 'smaller' criminal names and their investigations out to the suburban police regions, people like Mehmet Arif, George Davis, Freddie Foreman, Mickey McAvoy etc. were shifted off the books of the Met. so his force could catch the bigger criminals they were now faced with. A lot of the Flying Squad took early retirement as the investigations by a tranche of new officers brought in from the rural forces delved into the tie-ups between the Met's force and criminals.

On 9 February 1970 Bertie Smalls led a team of robbers known as The Wembley Mob, including Mickey Green, on an insider-led raid on a branch of Barclays Bank at 144 High Road, Ilford. The gang got away with £237,736, a record at the time. Most of the team left England via various routes – Smalls went via ferry from Newhaven to Dieppe, train to Paris and then a flight to Torremolinos. Most headed for the Costa del Sol where they hid from view and read the English newspapers for updates on the police search for them.

After making an early breakthrough where an informant provided the names of every member of the gang the police gave the impression the case had cooled to tempt the robbers back to Britain. The ruse worked and one by one they returned. Smalls was caught in a suburb of Northampton and spent Christmas in police custody in London.

On 2 January, Smalls asked for a meeting with the lead Inspector of the case and in the conversation Smalls (having been informed by his solicitor that he would be serving at least 25 years if convicted) offered the police a deal to name and incriminate those involved not only in the Barclays Bank job but in every piece of criminal activity he had ever been involved with or known of if they offered him a deal. An agreement was drawn up between Smalls and the DPP, Sir Norman Skelhorn that gave Smalls immunity from prosecution in exchange for his help. Detective Superintendent Jack Slipper was involved in his debriefing and became Smalls handler from then on.

On 11 February 1974 the trial of the Wembley Mob in relation to the Barclays Bank robbery commenced at the Old Bailey, Court No.2.

Smalls gave evidence and assisted the authorities as promised and as he concluded his evidence against some of his former friends in one of the committal hearings, they sang to him from the dock the Vera Lynn song: We'll Meet Again, Don't Know Where, Don't Know When.....' which told smalls that a contract on his life had been placed.

On 20 May the trial finished, with the jury returning guilty verdicts on all participants two days later on 22 May. In total the judge handed out sentences totalling 106 years. In the following 14 months, Smalls's evidence convicted a further 21 crminals for a total of 308 years. Smalls also later ensured the release of Jimmy Saunders jailed by DCI Bert Wicksted for his part in the 1970 Ilford robbery, after a statement in which Smalls said Saunders was not part of the gang.

In the aftermath and after reflection on the Smalls deal, the Law Lords told the Director of Public Prosecutions that they found the arrangement with Smalls an 'unholy deal.' The outcome of this being that later super grasses, such as Maurice O'Mahoney, in 1974 then one of Britain's most violent armed robbers, who turned in more than 150 names in exchange for a much-reduced sentence, couldn't escape prison if they had committed serious crimes. O'Mahoney faced a minimum of 20 years but was sentenced eventually to 5 years.

The super grass system was taken to its pinnacle by a Metropolitan Police officer named DCI Tony Lundy known as the 'super grass master', running the system from Finchley offices. From 1977, Lundy often had four trials per week running but met his match in Michael 'Skinny' Gervaise, the leader of 24 March 1980 silver bullion robbery – then the largest in the UK. The team got away with 321 ingots of silver valued at £3.4 million which were being transferred from Samuel Montagu & Co Bank to Germany. After interviewing Gervaise the team were led on 4 June 1980 to a stack of 309 silver ingots. Gervaise later alleged that Lundy was close to Lennie Gibson (the pair were members of the same Boxing club), Gibson had supplied police uniforms for the raid via Lundy. Lundy was returned to the reformed Flying Squad and after a two-year investigation was fully cleared. In its conclusion to the Lundy report, the Police Authority concluded Lundy's team had got too close to the criminals. Evidence came for this from the statistics for armed robbery in the Metropolitan area. In 1972, the annual total of armed robberies in the Metropolitan district was 380 – the year after Smalls, it had reduced to 168. By 1978, it had risen to 734 and by 1982 it had more than doubled, to 1,772, a 366 percent increase in a decade. The Flying Squad was revived to centralize specialist robbery squads, improve technical surveillance and the provision of police tactical firearms units.

As part of his deal with the police, Smalls received a new identity. Within a few years of the trial he had returned to his old haunts in North London, drinking openly in the pubs around Hornsey and often boasting he was paid £25 a week by Scotland Yard for his betrayal. He died in January 2008 at his home in Croydon.

Bobby King, one of the robbers his evidence convicted and who was later held up as an example of the positive side of prison, once saw him in Crouch End and said he saw it as a test of his own rehabilitation working that he didn't whack Smalls.

In 1988 DCSI Tony Lundy retired aged 49 to the Costa

Del Sol for a quiet retirement; one of his close neighbours out there and golfing partner was Mickey Green – by then Britain's most wanted criminal and biggest hard drug dealer. In 2005 the UK Government passed the Serious Organised Crime act which includes a 'tariff' for informants. Small's name lives on in the criminal world with even today people who grass about minor things are said to be 'doing a Bertie Smalls'.

On January 31, 2008, Bertie Smalls died at the age of 72, surprisingly of natural causes and not a bullet as he was the subject of a £1m contract with several signatures on it including the Krays. He was still under police witness protection at the time of his death. Although Smalls was generally described as Britain's first super grass, the former Scotland Yard detective Leonard 'Nipper' Read always maintained that Leslie Payne, the adviser to the Kray twins, who gave evidence against them in 1969, should have had that title.

However, Smalls certainly set the tone, and many of his former associates soon followed suit once the taboo had been broken. Few of them were given such a favourable deal, most getting five years, as opposed to the 18 or more they would otherwise have received for their crimes.

A short, squat man, described by a former colleague as like Bob Hoskins but without the charm, he held extreme right wing views and at the time of his arrest was knocking back a bottle of vodka a day. He was reviled throughout the criminal fraternity. One of the men he helped to convict spent many hours in jail teaching his pet budgie to say 'Bertie Smalls is a fucking grass.' But from the police point of view, Smalls was a godsend as he helped to jail many bank robbers who had escaped convictions by paying off corrupt officers during the early 1970s.

****

CHAPTER 11
1963 THE GREAT TRAIN ROBBERY.

The Great Train Robbery was the robbery of substantial sums of money from a Royal Mail train heading between Glasgow and London in the early hours of Thursday 8 August 1963 at Bridego Railway Bridge, Ledburn near Mentmore in Buckinghamshire. It is probably the one robbery that everyone knows about and kept the population glued to their television and radio news programs for weeks. After tampering with line signals, a 15-strong gang of robbers led by Bruce Reynolds (see his section) attacked the train. Other gang members included Gordon Goody, Buster Edwards, Charlie Wilson, Roy James, John Daly, Jimmy White, Ronnie Biggs, Tommy Wisbey, Jim Hussey, Bob Welch and Roger Cordrey as well as three men known only as numbers '1', '2' and '3'. A 16th man, an unnamed retired train driver, was also present at the time of robbery.

With careful planning based on inside information from an individual known as 'The Ulsterman' (named as Patrick McKenna in 2014), the robbers got away with over £2.6 million (the equivalent of £55 million today). The bulk of the stolen money was never recovered. The gang did not use any firearms but Jack Mills, the train driver, was beaten over the head with a metal bar. Mills' injuries were severe enough to end his career. After the robbery the gang hid at Leatherslade Farm. It was after the police found this hideout that incriminating evidence would lead to the eventual arrest and conviction of most of the gang because those who had been paid to clean the farm hadn't done their job.

The plan to intercept and rob the overnight Glasgow to London mail train was based on information from Patrick McKenna, a postal worker from Salford, Manchester who had detailed knowledge of the amounts of money carried on Royal Mail trains. McKenna was introduced to two of the criminals who would carry out the raid — Gordon Goody and Buster Edwards by London solicitor's clerk Brian Field. His name was kept secret, and he was known to the robbers only as 'the Ulsterman'. The raid was devised over a period of months by a core team of five Goody, Edwards and Bruce Reynolds, with Charlie Wilson and Roy James, Reynolds assumed the role of team leader This gang, although very successful in the criminal underworld, had virtually no experience in stopping and robbing trains. So it was agreed to enlist the help of another London gang called 'The South Coast

Raiders'. This group, which included Tommy Wisbey, Bob Welch and Jim Hussey, who were already accomplished train robbers, also included Roger Cordrey a man who was a specialist in this field and knew how to rig the trackside signals to stop the train. Other associates (including Ronnie Biggs, a man Reynolds had previously met in jail) were added as the plan evolved and the final gang who took part in the raid comprised a total of 16 men.

At 6:50 pm on Wednesday 7 August 1963, the travelling post office (TPO) Up Special train set off from Glasgow Central Station *en route* to Euston Station in London. It was scheduled to arrive at Euston at 3:59 am the following morning. The train was hauled by an English Electric type 4 (later Class 40) diesel-electric locomotive D326 (later 40 126). The train consisted of 12 carriages and carried 72 Post Office staff who sorted mail during the journey. Mail was loaded onto the train at Glasgow and also during station stops *en route*, and from line-side collection points where local post office staff would hang mail sacks on elevated track-side hooks that were caught by nets deployed by the on-board staff. Sorted mail on the train could be dropped off at the same time. This process of exchange allowed mail to be distributed locally without delaying the train with unnecessary stops. One of the carriages involved in the robbery is preserved at the Nene Valley Railway. The second carriage behind the engine was known as the HVP (High Value Packages) coach, which carried large quantities of money and registered mail for sorting. Usually the value of the shipment was in the region of £300,000, but because there had been a Bank Holiday weekend in Scotland, the total on the day of the robbery was to be between £2.5 and £3 million. In 1960, the Post Office Investigation Branch (IB) recommended the fitting of alarms to all Travelling Post Offices with HVP carriages. This recommendation was implemented in 1961, but HVP carriages without alarms were retained in reserve. By August 1963, three HVP carriages were equipped with alarms, bars over the windows and bolts and catches on the doors, but at the time of the robbery these carriages were out of service, so a reserve carriage (M30204M) without those features had to be used. The fitting of radios was also considered but they were deemed to be too expensive and the measure was not implemented. The actual robbed carriage was kept for evidence for seven years following the event and then burned at a scrap yard in Norfolk in the presence of police and post office officials to deter any souvenir hunters.

Just after 3:00 am on the 8th of August, the driver, Jack Mills from Crewe, stopped the train on the West Coast Main Line at a red signal light at Sears Crossing, Ledburn, between Leighton Buzzard in Bedfordshire and Cheddington in Buckinghamshire. The signal had been tampered with by the robbers who had covered the green light and connected a six-volt battery to power the red light. The locomotive's second crew-member, known as the second man or fireman, was 26-year-old David Whitby, also from Crewe. He climbed down from the cab to call the signalman from a railway track-side telephone, only to find the cables had been cut. As he made his return to the train, he was grabbed from behind and quickly overpowered by one of the robbers. Meanwhile, the train driver, 58- year-old Mills, waited in the cab for Whitby's return. Gang members entered the cabin from both sides of the train and as Mills grappled with one robber and attempted to force him off the footplate, he was struck from behind by another gang member with a cosh, rendering him semi-conscious. At this stage the robbers had foreseen that they would encounter a problem. They had to move the train from where it had been stopped to a suitable place to load their ex-army drop side truck with the stolen money. Bridge No.127 (Bridego Bridge, now known as Mentmore Bridge), approximately half a mile further along the track was the chosen location. One of the robbers (masquerading as a school teacher) had spent months befriending railway staff and familiarizing himself with the layout and operation of trains and carriages. Ultimately though it was decided that it would be better to use an experienced train driver to move the locomotive and the first two carriages from the rigged signals to the bridge after uncoupling them from the other carriages containing the rest of the sorters and the ordinary mail. On the night, the gang's hired train driver, an acquaintance of Ronnie Biggs, later referred to as 'Stan Agate' or 'Peter', was unable to operate this newer type of locomotive; although having driven trains for many years (then retired), he was experienced only on shunting (switching) locomotives on

the Southern Region. With no other alternative available to them, it was quickly decided that the original driver, Mills would have to move the train to the stopping point near the bridge, which was indicated by a white sheet stretched between poles on the track. Biggs only task was to supervise "Stan Agate's" participation in the robbery, and when it became obvious that Agate was not able to drive the train he and Biggs were sent to the waiting truck to help load the mail bags. (Biggs made a fortune telling the story of this heist with books, TV and film payments but the truth is he was a very petty villain and wife beater and the only reason he was in the team was because he said he knew a retired driver that the gang needed to move the train.)

The train was stopped at Bridego Bridge, and the gang attacked the High Value Packages (HVP) carriage. Frank Dewhurst was in charge of the three other postal workers (Leslie Penn, Joseph Ware and John O'Connor) in the HVP carriage. Thomas Kett, assistant inspector in charge of the train from Carlisle to Euston was also in the carriage. Dewhurst and Kett were hit with coshes when they made a vain attempt to prevent the robbers' storming of the carriage. Once the robbers had entered the carriage, the staff could put up no effective resistance and there was no police officer or security guard on board to assist them. They were made to lie face down on the floor in a corner of the carriage. Mills and Whitby were then brought into the carriage, handcuffed together and lay down beside the staff.

The robbers removed all but eight of the 128 sacks from the HVP carriage, which they transferred in about 15–20 minutes to the waiting truck by forming a human chain. They departed some 30 minutes after the robbery had begun in their Austin Loadstar truck and in an effort to mislead any potential witnesses, they used two Land Rover vehicles, both of which had the registration plates BMG 757A.They headed along minor roads listening for police broadcasts on a VHF radios, the journey taking somewhere between 45 minutes and an hour, and arrived back at Leatherslade Farm at around 4:30 am, this was about the same time as the first reports of the crime were being made. Leatherslade was a run-down farm 27 miles (43 km) from the crime scene between Oakley and Brill in Buckinghamshire . It had been bought two months earlier as their hideout.

At the farm they counted the proceeds and divided it into 16 full shares and several 'drinks' (smaller sums of money intended for associates of the gang who had helped in buying the farm, stealing the vehicles etc but weren't present at the robbery). The precise amounts of the split differ according to the source, but the full shares came to approximately £150,000 each (about £3 million today). From listening to their police-tuned radio, the gang learned that the police had calculated they had gone to ground within a 30-mile radius of the crime scene rather than dispersing with their haul. This declaration was based on information given by a witness at the crime scene who stated that a gang member had told the post office workers 'not to move for half an hour'. The press interpreted this information as a 30-mile (48 km) radius which was a half-hour drive in a fast car. The gang realised the police were using a net tactic, starting with a ring of officers at the robbery scene and working out for thirty miles searching any and every building they came on, and with help from the public, would probably discover the farm much sooner than had been originally anticipated. As a result, the plan for leaving the farm was brought forward to Friday from Sunday (the crime was committed on Thursday). The vehicles they had driven to the farm could no longer be used because they had been seen by the train staff. BrianField came to the farm on Thursday to pick up his share of the loot and to take Roy James to London to find an extra vehicle. Bruce Reynolds and John Daly picked up cars, one for Jimmy White and the other for Reynolds, Daly, Biggs and the replacement train driver. Field, his wife Karin and his associate 'Mark' brought the vans and drove the remainder of the gang to the Fields's home to rest and plan the next move. Field had arranged with 'Mark' to carry out a comprehensive clean- up and set fire to the farm after the robbers had left, even though the robbers had already spent much time wiping the place down to be free of prints. According to Buster Edwards, he 'nicked' £10,000

in ten shilling notes to help pay 'Mark's' drink. However, on Monday, when Charlie Wilson rang Brian Field to check whether the farm had been cleaned, he did not believe Field's assurances. He called a meeting with Edwards, Reynolds, Daly and James and they agreed that they needed to be sure. They called Field to a meeting on Tuesday, where he was forced to admit that he had failed to 'torch' the farm. In the IVS 2012 documentary film *The Great Train Robbery*, Nick Reynolds (son of Bruce Reynolds) says ' …the guy who was paid to basically go back to the farm and burn it down did a runner with his share.' Wilson would have killed Field there and then but was restrained by the others. By the time they were ready to go back to the farm, however, they learned that police had found already found it.

There is some uncertainty regarding the exact cash total stolen from the train. £2,631,684 is a figure quoted in the press at the time, although the police investigation states the theft as £2,595,997 10s, in 636 packages, contained in 120 mailbags, most of it in £1 and £5 notes (both the older white note and the newer blue note of the time, which was half its size). There were also ten-shilling notes and Irish and Scottish money. Because a 30-minute time limit had been set by Reynolds to unload the train, eight out of 128 bags were not stolen and were left behind. Statistically, this could have amounted to £131,000 or 4.7% of the total. It is alleged that the total weight of the bags removed was 2.5 tons according to former Buckinghamshire police officer John Woolley.

The robbers had cut all the telephone lines in the vicinity, but one of the rail-men left on the train at Sears Crossing stopped a passing goods train and rode it to Cheddington, where he raised the alarm at around 4:20 am. The first reports of the robbery were broadcast on the VHF police radio within a few minutes and this is where the gang heard the line 'A robbery has been committed and you'll never believe it – they've stolen the train!'

The gang consisted of 17 full members who were to receive an equal share, including the men who were at the robbery and two key informants. The men that carried out the actual robbery consisted of 15 criminals predominantly from south London: Gordon Goody, Charlie Wilson, Buster Edwards, Bruce Reynolds, Roy James, John Daly, Roger Cordrey, Jimmy White, Bob Welch, Tommy Wisbey, Jim Hussey, Ronnie Biggs, as well as Harry Smith and Danny Pembroke, who were never charged due to the lack of evidence against them, and one still unknown, plus the train driver they nicknamed 'Pop'. The best known member of the gang, Biggs, had only a minor role—to recruit the train driver.

Bruce Richard Reynolds   was born on 7 September 1931 at

53

Charing X Hospital, The Strand, London, to Thomas Richard and Dorothy Margaret (née Keen). His mother died in 1935, and he had trouble living with his father and stepmother, and often stayed with one or other of his grandmothers. Reynolds was jailed for three years on several counts of breaking and entering, and upon his release quickly started re-offending. He soon joined a gang with future best friend Harry Booth and future brother-in-law John Daly. Later on, he did some work with Jimmy White and met Buster Edwards at one of Charlie Richardson's clubs in South London. Richardson in turn introduced him to Gordon Goody. After the train heist, Reynolds escaped to Mexico with his wife, Angela, and young son, Nick Reynolds (who later became a member of the band Alabama 3, whose song "Woke Up This Morning" is the opening theme of The Sopranos TV series). He lived lavishly with his share of the take, approximately 150,000 British pounds. When that money ran out, Reynolds moved his family to Canada and then France under false identities, in search of work, before returning to the United Kingdom to pursue opportunities promised by his old criminal contacts. He was arrested in 1968 in rented accommodation in Torquay and sentenced to 25 years in jail. He was released a decade later. Reynolds was re-incarcerated in the mid-1980s for dealing amphetamines. In a 2003 interview, he recalls 'from an early age I always wanted a life of adventure.' He was rejected by the Royal Navy because of poor eyesight, and then tried to become a foreign correspondent, but his highest achievement in that vein was to become a clerk at the Daily Mail tabloid offices. While his life in crime did provide excitement, Reynolds said in 2003, 'I've always felt that I can't escape my past. And in many ways I feel that it is like a line from the Ancient Mariner and that the notoriety was like an albatross around my neck.' Reynolds died aged 81 on 28 February 2013 after a brief illness. He is survived by his son Nick.

Douglas Gordon Goody was regarded as the mastermind of the operation by the authorities. He first made contact with 'The Ulsterman' in a meeting set up by Brian Field in Finsbury Park. Of Northern Irish descent, Goody was born in Putney, London in March 1930 and was still living there in his mother's flat at the time of the robbery. In the early 1960s he joined Buster Edwards' gang and helped rob various easy targets. In September 2014, Goody revealed the identity of 'The Ulsterman' as Patrick McKenna for the first time. Revealing of the name coincided with a documentary marking the 50th anniversary of the robbery. The documentary makers employed Ariel Bruce (a social worker who finds missing family members) to trace Patrick McKenna, who was found to have died some years previously. However Bruce was able to make contact with McKenna's family who were unaware of their father's involvement and had never enjoyed any financial benefits in their life. This documentary was shown in cinemas and on demand in October 2014. Gordon Goody died in Spain where he owned a bar on 30th January 2016

Charles Frederick (Charlie) Wilson The most dangerous of the Great Train Robbers was 'the Silent Man' Charlie Wilson. He was born on 30th June 1932 to Bill and Mabel Wilson in Battersea, London. His friends from childhood were Jimmy Hussey, Tommy Wisbey, Bruce Reynolds and Gordon Goody. Later on, he met Ronald 'Buster' Edwards and the young driving enthusiasts Mickey Ball and Roy James, who had taken up car theft. From 1948 to 1950 he was called up for national service, and in 1955 he married Patricia Osborne, with whom he had three children. He turned to crime early in life. Whilst he did have legitimate work in his in-laws' grocer's shop, he was also a thief and his criminal proceeds went into buying shares in various gambling enterprises. He went to jail for short spells for numerous offences. In 1960, he began to work with Bruce Reynolds and planned to get into the criminal big league.

Ronald "Buster" Edwards Ronald Christopher Edwards was born on 27th January 1932 at Lambeth, London, the son of a barman. After leaving school, he worked in a sausage factory, where he began his criminal career by stealing meat to sell on the post-war black market. During his national service in the RAF he was detained for stealing cigarettes. When he returned to South London, he ran a drinking club and became a professional criminal. He married June Rose in 1952. They had a daughter, Nicky

Brian Field Brian Arthur Field was born on 15 December 1934 and was immediately put up for adoption. He served two years in the Royal Army Service Corps, seeing service during the KoreanWar. Although soldiers in the Service Corps were considered combat personnel they were primarily associated with transport and logistics.

When he was discharged from the military it was with 'a very good character' report. Field later became a solicitor's managing clerk for John Wheater & Co. Although he was only 28 at the time of the robbery, he was already apparently more prosperous than his boss, John Wheater. Field drove a new Jaguar and had a house named 'Kabri' an amalgam of Karin and Brian Field, at the Bridle Path, Whitchurch Hill, Oxfordshire, while his boss owned a battered Ford and lived in a run-down neighbourhood. Part of the reason for Field's prosperity was that he was not averse to giving Goody and Edwards information about what his clients had in their country houses, making them prime targets for the thieves. On one occasion he described the contents and layout of a house near Weybridge where wife Karin had once been a nanny. Prior to the robbery Field had represented Buster Edwards and Gordon Goody. He had arranged Edward's defence when he had been caught with a stolen car and had met Goody at a nightclub in Soho. Field was called upon to assist in Goody's defence in the aftermath of the "Airport Job", which was a robbery carried out on 27 November 1962 at a branch of Barclays Bank at London Heathrow Airport. This was the big practice robbery that the South West Gang had done before the Great Train Robbery. Field was successful in arranging bail for both Goody and Charlie Wilson.

The Ulsterman In 2014, Douglas Gordon Goody revealed to journalists the name of *The Ulsterman* as Patrick McKenna, a 43- year-old postal worker living in Salford, Manchester at the time of the robbery. McKenna, who was from Belfast, met Goody four times in 1963. Goody alleges he only found out McKenna's name when he saw it written inside his spectacles case.It is not known what became of the share McKenna received but his children were 'flabbergasted' upon hearing of their father's involvement. It was surmised that McKenna either donated his share to the Catholic Church over the years or had had the money stolen from him.

William Gerald Boal (22 October 1913 – 26 June 1970), an accomplice after the robbery of Roger Cordrey. He was wrongly convicted as being one of the robbers, despite playing a role no different to the many other accomplices of the various train robbers. Boal tragically died in jail.

Leonard Denis Field (born 1931, date of death unknown helped with the purchase of Leatherslade Farm paying the deposit of 5,000 pounds in return for a 'drink' of £12,000. Lennie was allowed to think that the plan was to hijack a lorry load of cigarettes. Despite not being in on the robbery, he was convicted and sentenced to 25 years (20 years for conspiracy to rob and 5 years for obstructing justice).

John Denby Wheater (born 17 December 1921, died July 1985), was the employer of Brian Field. He was convicted and sentenced to 3 years.

At 5am on the morning after the robbery, Chief Superintendent Malcolm Fewtrell, head of the Buckinghamshire Police Criminal Investigation Department (CID), located at Aylesbury, arrived at the crime scene, where he supervised evidence-gathering. He then went to Cheddington Railway Station, where the train had been taken, and where statements were being taken from the driver and postal workers. As I said earlier a member of the gang had made the mistake of telling the postal staff not to move for half an hour and this suggested to the police that their hide-out could not be more than 30 miles (48 km) away. It appeared, from interviews with the witnesses, that about 15 hooded men dressed in blue boiler suits had been involved, but little more could be gleaned. By lunchtime of the following day, it became obvious to Fewtrell that extra resources were needed to cope with the scale of the investigation and the Buckinghamshire Chief Constable referred the case to Scotland Yard. George Hatherill, Commander of the C Department and Detective Chief Superintendent Earnest (Ernie) Millen, Head of the Flying Squad were initially in charge of the London side of the investigation. They sent Detective Superintendent Gerald McArthur and Detective Sergeant John Pritchard to assist the Buckinghamshire Police. The police then undertook a major search, spreading out from the crime scene after having failed to find any forensic evidence there. A watch was put on the seaports and airports. The Post Office offered a £10,000 reward to 'the first person giving information leading to the apprehension and conviction of the persons responsible for the robbery'.

Following a tip-off from a herdsman who used a field adjacent to Leatherslade Farm, a police sergeant and constable called there on 13th August 1963, five days after the robbery. The farm was deserted but they found the truck used by the robbers, which had been hastily painted yellow, as well as the two Land Rovers. They also found a large quantity of food, bedding, sleeping bags, post-office sacks, registered mail packages, banknote wrappers and a Monopoly Board Game. It was determined that although the farm had been cleaned for fingerprints by the gang, some finger and palm prints (presumably of the robbers) had been overlooked, including those on a ketchup bottle and on the Monopoly set (which had been used after the robbery for a game, but with real money). Despite the discovery of Leatherslade Farm, the investigation was not going very slowly. The London side of the investigation then continued under Detective Chief Superintendent Tommy Butler, who replaced Ernest Millen as head of the Flying Squad shortly after Millen was promoted to Deputy Commander under George Hatherill. On Monday 12th August 1963, Butler was appointed to head the police investigation of the London connection and quickly formed a six-man Train Robbery Squad. With Leatherslade Farm finally found on 13th August 1963, the day after Tommy Butler was appointed to head the London investigation, the Train Robbery Squad descended on the farm. The key breakthrough was when Detective Chief Superintendent Millen met a distinguished barrister in a smoking room of an exclusive West End club and was told that someone was willing to inform on the gang. The process of talking to the informer was handled by Hatherill and Millen themselves, and they never divulged the identity of the informer to the detectives in their command. The informant had just been jailed in a provincial jail before the train robbery, and was hoping to get parole and his sentence reduced from talking. He clearly did not know all the names and a second informant (a woman) was able to fill in the gaps. Millen stated in his book Specialist in Crime, 'the break through with the informer came at a moment when I and my colleagues at the Yard were in a state of frustration almost approaching despair'. This process saw them get 18 names to be passed on to detectives to match up with the list being prepared from fingerprints collected at Leatherslade. Unfortunately, the decision to publish photos of the wanted suspects had already been made by Hatherill and Millen despite strong protests from Tommy Butler and Frank Williams. This resulted in most of the robbers quickly going to ground. Tommy Butler was a shrewd choice to take over the Flying Squad and in particular the Train Robbery

Squad. He became arguably the most renowned head of the Flying Squad in its history. He was known variously as 'Mr Flying Squad' or 'One-day Tommy' for the speed with which he apprehended criminals and as the 'Grey Fox' for his shrewdness. He was Scotland Yard's most formidable thief-taker and, as an unmarried man who still lived with his mother, he had a fanatical dedication to the job. Butler worked long hours and expected all members of the squad to do the same. The squad later had to work out rotations whereby one member would go home to rest as otherwise they were getting only three hours of sleep per night and had no time to eat healthily or see their families. When the squad tried to get him to ease the working conditions, Butler was enraged and threatened to send them back to their normal duties.

Butler was said to be very secretive, with Jack Slipper claiming in his book *Slipper of the Yard* (1981) that "he wouldn't even tell his own left hand what the right one was doing". This meant that Train Robbery Squad members were often dispatched on specific errands with no knowledge of how their tasks fitted into the overall investigation.

The six-man squad of detectives assigned to the robbery were Detective Inspector Frank Williams, Detective Sergeant Steve Moore, Detective Sergeant Jack Slipper, Detective Sergeant Jim Nevill, Detective Sergeant Lou Van Dyck and Detective Constable Tommy Thorburn. The senior officer, Frank Williams, was a quiet man. His speciality was dealing with informants and he had the best working knowledge of the South London criminal fraternity in the force. One of the squad, Jack Slipper, would later become head of the Flying Squad and would still be involved in the case many years later.

The Post Office Investigation Branch (IB) was tasked with immediately establishing the amount of money stolen, which they uded totaled to £2,595,997.10s.0d. They also sought to identify what money had been taken so that the relevant banks could be notified. The installation of radios in the HVP carriages was recommended as a priority.This investigation was detailed in a report by Assistant Controller Richard Yates that was issued in May 1964

Roger Cordrey The first gang member to be caught was Roger Cordrey. He was with his friend, William Boal, who was helping him lay low in return for the payment of old debts. They were living in a rented, fully furnished flat above a florist's shop in Wimborne Road,

Mooredown, Bournemouth. The Bournemouth police were tipped off by police widow Ethel Clark, when Boal and Cordrey paid rent for a garage (in Tweedale Road off Castle Lane West), three months in advance, all in used ten-shilling notes. William Boal, who was not involved in the robbery, was sentenced to 24 years and died in prison in 1970. Police later acknowledged that he was the victim of a miscarriage of justice. Other arrests followed. Eight of the gang members and several associates were caught. The other arrests were made by Sergeant Stan Davis and Probationary Constable Gordon Chase. On Friday 16 August 1963, two people who had decided to take a morning stroll in Dorking Woods discovered a briefcase, a holdall and a camel-skin bag, all containing money. They called the police, who also discovered another briefcase full of money in the woods. In total, a sum of £100,900 was found. They also found a camel-skin bag with a receipt inside from the Cafe Pension Restaurant, Sonnenbichel, Hindelang, Province of Allgua. It was made out in favour of a Herr and Frau Field. The Surrey police delivered the money and the receipt to Fewtrell and McArthur in Aylesbury, who knew by then that Brian Field was a clerk at James & Wheater who had acted in the purchase of Leatherslade Farm. They quickly confirmed through Interpol that Brian and Karin Field had stayed at the Pension Sonnebichel in February that year. In addition, they knew that Field had acted for Gordon Goody and other criminals in several cases. Some weeks later, the police went to "Kabri" to interview Field, who calmly provided a cover story that implicated Lennie Field as the purchaser of the farm and his boss John Wheater as the conveyancer. He admitted to visiting the farm on one occasion with Lennie Field, but said he assumed it was an investment of his brother. Brian Field, not knowing the police had found a receipt, readily confirmed that he and his wife had been to Germany on a holiday and gave them the details of the place at which they had stayed. On 15th September 1963 Brian Field was arrested and his boss John Wheater was arrested two days later. Lennie Field had already been arrested on 14 September. Meanwhile Detective Jack Slipper was arresting Roy James, Ronald Biggs, Jimmy Hussey and John Daly.

The trial of the robbers began at Aylesbury Assizes, Buckinghamshire, on 20th January 1964. Because it would be necessary to accommodate a large number of lawyers and journalists, the existing court was far too small and so the offices of Aylesbury Rural District Council were specially converted for the event. The defendants were brought to the court each day from Aylesbury Prison in a compartmentalised van, out of view of the large crowd of spectators. Mr Justice Edmund Davies presided over the trial, which lasted 51 days and included 613 exhibits and 240 witnesses. The jury retired to the Grange Youth Centre in Aylesbury to consider their verdict. On 11th February 1964, there was a sensation when John Daly was found to have no case to answer. His counsel, Mr Raeburn QC, claimed that the evidence against his client was limited to his fingerprints being on the Monopoly set found at Leatherslade farm and the fact that he went underground after the robbery. Raeburn went on to say that Daly had played the Monopoly game with his brother-in-law Bruce Reynolds earlier in 1963, and that he had gone underground only because he was associated with people publicly sought by the police. This was not proof of involvement in a conspiracy. The judge agreed, and the jury was directed to acquit him. Detective Frank Williams was shocked when this occurred because, owing to Tommy Butler's refusal to share information, he had no knowledge of the fact that Daly's prints were only on the Monopoly set. If Williams had known this, he could have asked Daly questions about the Monopoly set and robbed him of his very effective alibi. Daly was clever in avoiding having a photo taken when he was arrested until he could shave his beard. This meant that there was no photo to show the lengths he had gone to, to change his appearance. On 15th April 1964 the proceedings ended with the judge describing the robbery as 'a crime of sordid violence inspired by vast greed' and passing sentences of 30 years' imprisonment on seven of the robbers.

The eleven men sentenced all felt aggrieved at the sentences handed down, particularly Bill Boal (who died in prison) and Lennie Field, who were later found not guilty of the charges against them. The other men (aside from Wheater) resented what they considered to be the excessive length of the sentences, which were longer than those given to many murderers or armed robbers at the time. At that period, there was no parole system in place and prisoners served the full term of the sentence. Train robbers who were sentenced later, and by different judges, received shorter terms. At the time, the severity of the sentences caused some surprise and it was felt that the then crumbling Conservative government, still reeling from the Profumo/Keeler scandal, had instructed the judge to give the impression that they were still on top of things generally. When he was arrested in 1968, the mastermind Bruce Reynolds is said to have told the arresting officer Tommy Butler, that those sentences had had a detrimental effect. According to him, they had prompted criminals generally to take guns with them when they set out on robberies.

Ronald Arthur Biggs	4	carpenter	30 years (25 years for conspiracy to rob and 30 years for armed robbery)
Douglas Gordon Goody	4	hairdresser	30 years (25 years for conspiracy to rob and 30 years for armed robbery)
Charles Frederick Wilson	1	market trader	30 years (25 years for conspiracy to rob and 30 years for armed robbery)
Thomas William Wisbey	4	bookmaker	30 years (25 years for conspiracy to rob and 30 years for armed robbery)
Robert Welch	4	club proprietor	30 years (25 years for conspiracy to rob and 30 years for armed robbery)
James Hussey	4	painter	30 years (25 years for conspiracy to rob and 30 years for armed robbery)
RoyJohn James	8	racing motorist and silversmith	30 years (25 years for conspiracy to rob and 30 years for armed robbery)

Roger John Cordrey	2	florist	20 years (20 years for conspiracy to rob and various receiving stolen goods charges)
Brian Arthur Field	9	solicitor's clerk	25 years (20 years for Conspiracy to rob and 5 years for obstructing justice)
Leonard Denis Field	1	merchant seaman	25 years (20 years for Conspiracy to rob and 5 years for obstructing justice)
John Denby Wheater	1	solicitor	3 years
William Gerald Boal	0	engineer	24 years

On 13 July 1964, the appeals by Lennie Field and Brian Field (no relation) against the charges of conspiracy to rob were allowed. This meant that their sentences were effectively reduced to five years only. On 14 July 1964, the appeals by Roger Cordrey and Bill Boal were allowed, with the convictions for conspiracy to rob quashed, leaving only the receiving charges. Justice Fenton Atkinson concluded that a miscarriage of justice would result if Boal's charges were upheld, given that his age, physique and temperament made him an unlikely train robber. Luckily for him, as the oldest robber, Cordrey was also deemed to be not guilty of the conspiracy because his prints had not been found at Leatherslade Farm. Brian Field was only reluctantly acquitted of the robbery. Justice Atkinson stated that he would not be surprised if Field were not only part of the conspiracy, but also one of the robbers. The charges against the other men were all upheld. In the end Lennie Field and Bill Boal got some measure of justice, but Boal died in prison in 1970 after a long illness.

On 12th August 1964, Wilson escaped from Winson Green Prison in Birmingham in under three minutes, the escape being considered unprecedented in that a three-man team had broken into the prison to extricate him. His escape team was never caught and the leader, nicknamed 'Frenchy', had disappeared from the London criminal scene by the late 1960s. Two weeks after his escape Wilson was in Paris for plastic surgery. By November 1965, Wilson was in Mexico visiting old friends Bruce Reynolds and Buster Edwards. Wilson's escape was yet another dramatic twist in the train robbery saga. Eleven months after Wilson's escape, in July 1965, Biggs escaped from Wandsworth Prison, 15 months into his sentence. A furniture van was parked alongside the prison walls and a ladder was dropped over the 30-foot-high wall into the prison during outside exercise time, allowing four prisoners to escape, including Biggs. The escape was planned by recently released prisoner Paul Seaborne with the assistance of two other ex-convicts, Ronnie Leslie and Ronnie Black, with support from Biggs' wife, Charmian. The plot saw two other prisoners interfere with the warders, and allow Biggs and friend Eric flower to escape. Seaborne was later caught by Detective Butler and sentenced to four-and-a-half years and Ronnie Leslie received three years for being the getaway driver. The two other prisoners who took advantage of the Biggs escape were captured after three months. Biggs and Flower paid a significant sum of money to be smuggled to Paris for plastic surgery. Biggs said he had to escape because of the length of the sentence and what he alleged to be the severity of the prison conditions. Wilson and Biggs' escape meant that five of the known robbers were now on the run, with DS Tommy Butler in hot pursuit.

With the other robbers on the run and having fled the country, only White was at large in the United Kingdom. White was a renowned locksmith/thief and had already been on the run for ten years before the robbery. He was said to have a remarkable ability to be invisible, to merge with his surroundings and become the ultimate Mr Nobody. He was a wartime paratrooper and a veteran of Arnhem. He was a solitary thief, not known to work with others, and should have had a good chance of remaining undetected altogether, yet was known to be one of the Train Robbers almost at once, first by other criminals and then by the police. He was unfortunate in that Brian Field's relatives had dumped luggage containing £100,000 only a mile from a site where White had bought a caravan and hidden £30,000 in the panelling. In addition, a group of men purporting to be from the Flying Squad broke into his flat and took a briefcase containing £8,500.

Throughout his three years on the run with wife Sheree and baby son Stephen, he was taken advantage of or let down by friends and associates. On 10 April 1966 a new friend recognised him from photos in a newspaper and informed police. They arrested him at Littlestone while he was at home. He only had £8,000 to hand back to them. The rest was long gone. He was tried in June 1966 at Leicester Assizes and Mr Justice Nield sentenced him to 18 years' jail, considerably less than the 30 years given to other principal offenders.

Buster Edwards fled to Mexico with his family, to join Bruce Reynolds (and later Charlie Wilson) but returned voluntarily to England in 1966, where he was sentenced to 15 years.

Charlie Wilson took up residence outside Montreal, Canada, on Rigaud Mountain in an upper-middle-class neighbourhood where the large, secluded properties are surrounded by trees. He lived under the name Ronald Alloway, a name borrowed from a Fulham shopkeeper. His wife and three children soon joined him. He joined an exclusive golf club and participated in the activities of the local community. It was only when he invited his brother-in-law over from the UK for Christmas that Scotland

Yard was able to track him down and recapture him. They waited three months before making their move in the hope that he would lead them to Reynolds, the last suspect still to be apprehended. Wilson was arrested on 25 January 1968 by DetectiveTommy Butler. Many in Rigaud, Canada petitioned that his wife and three daughters be allowed to stay in the Montreal area where he and they were now part of the community.

On 6 June 1964, Bruce Reynolds arrived in Mexico, with his wife Angela and son Nick joining him a few months later, after they evaded the obvious police surveillance. A year later in July 1965, Buster Edwards and his family arrived, although unlike the Reynolds they planned to return to England at some stage, and did not like Mexico. Charlie Wilson, on the run with his family back in England visited them for 6 weeks, so three of the train robbers were together in exile for a time. After the Edwards family returned to England, the Reynolds also decided to leave Mexico and go to Canada to potentially join up with the Wilson family, leaving on 6 December 1966. They had spent much of their share of the robbery by this point – living far more extravagantly than the Edwards had. After realizing the danger in settling near the Wilsons in Montreal, they went to live in Vancouver, and then went to Nice, France.

Reynolds did not want to go to Australia where Biggs was, and needing money decided to go back to England, settling briefly in Torquay before being captured by DetectiveTommy Butler.

Ronnie Biggs fled to Paris, where he acquired new identity papers and underwent plastic surgery. In 1970, he moved to Adelaide, Australia, where he worked as a builder and his wife had a third son. Tipped off of interest being shown by Interpol, he moved to Melbourne working as a set-constructor for TV Channel 9, later escaping to Rio de Janeiro, Brazil, after police had discovered his Melbourne address. Biggs could not be extradited because there was no extradition treaty between Britain and Brazil, and additionally he became father to a Brazilian son, which afforded him legal immunity. As a result, he lived openly in Rio for many years, safe from the British authorities. In 1981, Biggs' Brazilian son became a member of a successful band Turma do Balao Magico, but the band quickly faded into obscurity and dissolved. In May 2001, aged 71 and having suffered three strokes, Biggs voluntarily returned to England. Accepting that he could be arrested, his stated desire was to 'walk into a pub as an Englishman and buy a pint of bitter' Arrested on landing, after detention and a short court hearing he was sent back to prison to serve the remainder of his sentence. On 2 July 2009, Biggs was denied parole by Justice Secretary Jack Straw, who considered Biggs to be still 'wholly unrepentant.'

The Train Robbers are now mostly dead. In later years, the robbers generally came together only for the funerals of their fellow gang members. At Wilson's funeral on 10th May 1990, several attended, Bruce Reynolds saw Roy James (who got into a verbal argument with the press), Edwards, Welch (hobbling on crutches) and White (who went unnoticed most due to his ability to blend into the background). However at Edwards' funeral in 1994, Reynolds saw only Welch (Hussey, Wisbey and James were all in prison at the time).At Reynolds own funeral, only Welch and Biggs attended, both in wheelchairs, although a statement was read out on behalf of Gordon Goody.

After being sentenced on 16 April 1964, Brian Field

served four years of his five-year sentence. He was released in 1967. While he was in prison, his wife Karin divorced him and married a German journalist. Karin wrote an article for the German magazine Stern confirming that she took Roy James to Thame Station so he could go to London after the robbery and that she led a convoy of two vans back to 'Kabri', where the gang were joined by wives and girlfriends for a big party to celebrate the crime. When Reynolds returned to Great Britain in 1968, he tried to contact Field as this was the only way he could get in touch with the '*Ulsterman*'. It seems that Field was ambushed upon his release from prison by a recently released convict, 'Scotch' Jack Buggy, who presumably roughed up or even tortured Field with a view to extorting some of the loot from the robbery. Subsequently Field went to ground and Buggy was killed shortly after. Reynolds gave up trying to find Field. Field changed his name to Brian Carlton to disappear. Sometime after his release from prison, he married Welsh-born Sian. In the mid/late 1970s they worked for the Children's Book Centre (since sold) in Kensington High Street in London. Field and his wife Sian were responsible for the company's operations in central and southern Europe, to where they shipped English language books and held book fairs at international English schools. Field, aged 44, and Sian, aged 28, died in a car crash on the M4 motorway on 27th April 1979, a year after the last of the robbers had completed their sentences. The accident occurred as they returned from a visit to Sian's parents in Wales. A Mercedes driven by the pregnant 28-year-old daughter of well- known hairdresser Raymond Bessone (Mr Teasy Weasy) crossed a damaged section of the guard rail and slammed into Field's oncoming Porsche. The Fields, Teasy Weasy's daughter, her husband and two children were killed instantly. It was several weeks after the accident that Field's true identity was discovered. It is not clear whether his wife Sian ever knew of his past.

The last of the robbers released, (after serving about one-third of his sentence) Charlie Wilson returned to a life of crime and was found shot dead at his villa in Marbella, Spain, on 24 April 1990. His murder was thought to be related to suspected cheating in drug-dealing activity. He is buried in Streatham Cemetery.

After he was released Buster Edwards became a flower seller outside Waterloo Station. His story was dramatised in the 1988 film Buster, with Phil Collins in the title role. Edwards died in a garage in November 1994, allegedly committing suicide by hanging himself. His family continued to run the flower stall after his death.

Roy James went back to motor racing following his release on 15th August 1975. However, he crashed several cars so his chances of becoming a top driver quickly faded. After the failure of his sporting career, he returned to his trade as a silversmith. He produced the trophy given to Formula One promoters each year thanks to his acquaintance with Bernie Ecclestone. In 1982, he married a younger woman, but the marriage soon broke down. By 1983, James and Charlie Wilson had become involved in an attempt to import gold without paying excise duty. James was acquitted in January 1984 for his part in the swindle. In 1993, he shot and wounded his father-in-law, pistol-whipped and partially strangled his ex-wife. He was sentenced to six years in jail. In 1996, James underwent triple-bypass surgery and was subsequently released from prison in 1997, only to die almost immediately afterwards on 21st August after another heart attack. He was the fifth member of the gang to die, despite being the youngest.

Roger Cordrey was the first of the robbers to be released, but his share of the theft had almost entirely been recovered by the police.He went back to being a florist at his sister's business. He is now dead, and his son Tony has publicly acknowledged his dad confirmed that Bill Boal was innocent of any involvement in the robbery.

Bruce Reynolds, the last of the robbers to be caught, was released from prison on 6th June 1978 after serving 10 years. Reynolds, then aged 47, was helped by Gordon Goody to get back on his feet, before Goody departed for Spain. By October 1978, day-release ended and he had to report to a parole officer. Frank Monroe, one of the three robbers who were never caught, temporarily gave Reynolds a job, but did not want to attract undue attention by employing him for too long. Reynolds later got back together with his wife Angela and son Nicholas. He was arrested in 1983 for drug-related offences (Reynolds denied having any involvement). He was released again in March 1985 and dedicated himself to helping his wife recover from a mental breakdown. In 2001, he and his son Nicholas travelled with reporters from The Sun newspaper to bring Biggs back to Britain. In 2010, he wrote the postscript for *Signal Red*, Robert Ryan's novel based on the robbery, and he regularly commented on the robbery. He died in his sleep, aged 81, on 28 February 2013.

Upon his acquittal and release John Daly, found his share of the loot stolen and/or destroyed and gave up his life of crime and went 'straight'. He and his wife Barbara and their three children moved to Cornwall, where he worked as a street sweeper until the age of 70, known to the locals as Gentleman John or John the Gent. Daly told no one about the robbery as he was told he could face a retrial. He died 6 weeks after his brother in law Reynolds.

On 6th August 2009, Ronnie Biggs was granted release from prison on 'compassionate grounds', due to a severe case of pnuemonia and other ongoing health problems. Having suffered a series of strokes after his release, and unable to speak for the previous three years, Biggs died at the Carlton Court Care home, London on 18th December 2013.

Tommy Wisbey was luckier than most of the others, in that his loot had been entrusted to his brothers, and when he emerged, he had a house in South London and a few other investments to keep him going. Unfortunately, during his prison stint, his daughter Lorraine had died in a car accident. He took a while to learn how to live harmoniously with his wife Rene and his other daughter Marilyn moved out upon his return. Shortly after his release, Wisbey was imprisoned on remand over a swindle involving travellers' cheques. The judge acknowledged the minor nature of his role. Jimmy Hussey was released on 17 November 1975 and married girlfriend Gill (whom he had met just before the robbery). Hussey's share of the loot had been entrusted to a friend

of *Frank Monroe* who squandered it. Wisbey and Hussey fell back into crime together and were jailed in 1989 for cocaine dealing, with Wisbey sentenced to ten years and Hussey to seven years. In her book *Gangster's Moll*, Marilyn Wisbey recounts that on 8th June 1988, after returning home from a visit to an abortion clinic and lying down for a nap they were raided by the Drugs Squad. Her parents were staying with her and her son Jonathan while their tenants moved out of their house (they had been away on a long trip to the USA). The raid uncovered 1kilo of cocaine and Rene and Marilyn Wisbey were arrested along with Jimmy Hussey, who had been spotted accepting a package from Wisbey in a park. Wisbey himself was captured a year later in Wilmslow, Cheshire. He was allegedly staying with another woman, to the shock of his wife and daughter. In return for Hussey and Wisbey pleading guilty, the two women were unconditionally freed. Upon their release from prison, both men retired from work. Wisbey later said 'We were against drugs all our lives, but as the years went on, towards the end of the '70s, it became more and more the 'in' thing. Being involved in the Great Train Robbery, our name was good. They knew we had never grassed anyone, we had done our time without putting anyone else in the frame'. On 26 July 1989, the two men pleaded guilty and admitted at Snaresbrook Crown Court, London that they were a part of a £500,000 cocaine trafficking ring.

Bob Welch was released on 14th June 1976. He was the last of those convicted in Aylesbury to be released. Welch moved back in with his wife June and his son. He threatened the man left in charge of his share of the theft in order to retrieve the remainder. A leg injury sustained in prison forced him to undergo several operations, which left him semi-crippled.

Douglas (Gordon) Goody was released from prison on 23rd December 1975, aged 46 years old and went to live with his ill mother in her small cottage in Putney. Unlike the other robbers, he was exceptionally lucky in that the man he left in charge of his affairs was loyal and successful so he was able to live a relatively well-off life. In his final years of incarceration Goody had taken full benefit of the newly established education college at Wormwood Scrubs and studied Spanish to GCE standard. He later moved to Mojaca, Southern Spain, where he bought property and a bar and settled down, believing it safer to be out of the United Kingdom. He was at one point accused of cannabis smuggling but ultimately cleared.

The Ones Who Got Away - While there has been a lot of mystery surrounding several of the gang who were not imprisoned, in reality the police knew almost the entire gang almost instantly after the robbery. By 29th August 1963 Commander Hatherill had 14 names already, and told police that Brian Field had tried to enlist another gang to rob the train, who turned him down, Hatherill's list was unerringly accurate with all the major gang members that were later jailed identified on it, except Ronnie Biggs. With the exception of the minor accomplices Lennie Field, Bill Boal and the train driver, the list was complete, although of course the Ulsterman was not identified. In terms of the ones who got away, there were four others identified, Henry Smith, Dennis Pembroke, a fair haired man (25 years old well spoken, not named) and a Nondescript man (not named but may be Jimmy Collins) Both Piers Paul Read, and later Bruce Reynolds refer to three robbers who got away as Bill Jennings, Alf Thomas and Frank Monroe.

Bill 'Flossy' Jennings AKA Mr One   , Piers Paul Read refers to this man as Bill Jennings in *The Train Robbers*, while Bruce Reynolds adds a nickname – *Flossy*. Ronnie Biggs refers to him as Mr One, as do other accounts. According to Bruce Reynolds, 'Flossy had no previous convictions and stayed well out of contact with the group. A shadowy figure, nobody knew exactly where he lived or even what his real name was. All we knew that he was one hundred per cent, and was sure to last out the hullabaloo. The last report of him said that he was in a safe house, banged up with two gorgeous girls and enough champagne to float a battleship. It is clear that while Reynolds claims to not have known his real name that 'Flossy' was previously a core part of the gang who participated in the London Airport robbery. This robbery was the audacious raid that Gordon Goody and Charlie Wilson were acquitted of. That raid consisted of Roy James and Mickey Ball as the getaway drivers, with six robbers, Bruce Reynolds, Buster Edwards, Gordon Goody, Charlie Wilson, Flossy (and a sixth man who did not participate in the train robbery). In the end the only one caught after the airport raid was Mickey Ball, who pleaded guilty to being a getaway driver when a witness mistook him for Flossy, and to avoid being blamed for the actual violence he agreed to plead guilty as an accomplice, and was in prison during the Great Train Robbery. It is alleged that Henry Thomas 'Harry' Smith born 20 October 1930, was Flossy and unlike most other robbers, actually got to spend his share of the loot, buying 28 houses and also a hotel and drinking club in Portsmouth. Smith died in 2008 and was the only man not ultimately arrested that was on both the Hatherill and Tommy Butler lists.

Alf Thomas is alleged to have been a South Coast Raider, said to have been introduced by Jimmy White, which may have been true or a diversion by the robbers that told Read their story for his book. The man is sometimes referred to as Mr Two or Mr Three, depending on the account. Ronnie Biggs refers to him as Mr Three and notes several times that he is the biggest of the gang, and the one who stormed the cab to subdue the driver. It is alleged that he was Dennis (Danny) Pembroke. Following the robbery, Pembroke is said to have turned his back on crime and lived quietly in Kent, working as a cab driver. He died aged 79 from a heart attack at home and in his sleep on 28 February 2015. Pembroke had five children, and his son Danny Jnr, said his father had never spoken about the Great Train Robbery. Certainly he showed no signs of increased wealth afterwards, but as he allegedly gave up £47,245 of the money as part of a deal with Frank Williams, 1/3 of his share was already lost. On 6 September 1963, Flying Squad officers DCI Williams and Det Sgt Jack Slipper search Pembroke's house, but nothing incriminating was found and he was extensively interrogated and his prints taken. Samples of his pubic hair were taken to compare with those found in sleeping bags at Leatherslade Farm, but there was no match. The Flying Squad could therefore never prove that Danny Pembroke was one of the robbers as no forensic evidence linked him to the crime scene or the farm. After release, he went to the Devon village of Beaford with Welch with three others where locals became suspicious at the amount of £5 notes they were spending.

Frank Monroe According to Bruce Reynolds, Monroe, who was never caught, worked as a film stunt man for a while before starting a paper and scrap metal recycling business. Nothing is known of him after that.

The Replacement Train Driver AKA Pops/Dad, AKA Peter, AKA Stan Agate. The replacement train driver was never caught, and never suspected of even existing by police, due to the fact that Jack Mills in the end had to drive the train. He also never profited from the crime – Ronnie Biggs never paid him his £20,000 'drink'. He was not a member of the gang, as defined by receiving an equal share, just an accomplice. Piers Paul Read called the replacement train driver 'Stan Agate', and Stan was apparently the true nickname of the replacement driver. Read, concerned that the robbers may have hurt him, went to see Ronnie Biggs in Brazil to get his details, and found that Biggs did not know his last name and knew and cared very little about him. With the meagre details provided, Read used a detective agency to track down the driver at a town 20 miles south of London, and found that he was still alive, although somewhat senile and being cared for by his wife. The wife admitted that she had burnt all the clothes that he had worn that night, and had nervously waited for either the gang to murder him or the police to arrest him. Read promised not to reveal their identities.

Ronnie Biggs, in his 1994 autobiography, *Odd Man Out*, said that Bruce Reynolds offered to let him join the gang if he could find a train driver. Biggs was renewing the front windows of a train drivers' house in Redhill, who he calls 'Peter' and who he believes to be dead by 1994. Ronnie offers him a £40,000 share of the profits, and tells Reynolds and gives his address to John Daly who then proceeds to check him out. It seems that while he was an older man, he still had to apply for two weeks leave of absence from his job. According to Biggs, 'Peter' was paid his £40,000 'drink', although other accounts claim otherwise. Biggs states that Mary Manson drove 'Peter' and John Daly home, while Reynolds drove Biggs home. It is alleged in *The Sun* that the replacement train driver was Peter Stevens.

John Wheater, the solicitor, was released from prison on 11 February 1966 and managed his family's laundry business in Harrogate. He later wrote two articles in the *Sunday Telegraph*, who published the first one on 6 March 1966. Lenny Field was released in 1967 and went to live in North London. He disappeared from the public eye. Mary Manson, an associate of Bruce Reynolds and John Daly, was charged with receiving £820 from the robbery; she was held for six weeks but was released. Mary took care of wives and children of some of the robbers while they were on the run or in jail.

Much focus of the trial later press reporting, has been on the train driver Jack Mills, but Mills second man, David Whitby as well as other staff were attacked, and Whitby appears to have survived Mills by only a few years despite being younger.

Jack Mills had constant trauma headaches for the rest of his life. He died in 1970 from leukaemia. Mills' assailant was one of three members of the gang, who was never identified by the others. However, in November 2012, Hussey made a death-bed confession that it was him, although there were suspicions that this was repayment of a debt, to divert attention from the real perpetrator. Frank Williams, at the time a Detective Inspector, claims in the late 90s that at least three men who were directly involved were still at liberty and enjoying their full share of the money stolen and the profits from the way they invested it. One of them is the man responsible for the attack on the train driver. The train driver's assailant is not some phantom figure lurking in the criminal underworld. Williams traced him, identified him and took him to Scotland Yard where, with Tommy Butler, Williams questioned him. He could not be charged because of lack of evidence; there were no fingerprints or identifiable marks anywhere. None of those arrested informed on him although he had completely disobeyed instructions and used violence during the robbery.

David Whitby like Mills, was also from Crewe. He was traumatised by his track-side assault and subsequent rough treatment and never recovered from his ordeal. He was 25 years old at the time of the robbery. He was able to resume his railway career as a second man, but died from a heart attack on 6 January 1972 at the age of 34.

William Gerald Boal, 22nd October 1913 – 26 June 1970, an accomplice after the fact of Roger Cordrey, was wrongly convicted as being one of the robbers, despite playing a role no different to the many other accomplices of the various train robbers. Boal tragically died in jail of cancer. Boal's family tried to have his name cleared, as he clearly was at best an accomplice after the fact with no knowledge of the robbery, and Cordrey likely told him nothing about where he obtained the cash.

The audacity and scale of the robbery was yet another controversy with which the Conservative government of Harold Macmillan had to cope. Macmillan resigned in October 1963, claiming poor health. He had been diagnosed with prostate cancer and believed he did not have long to live, but the diagnosis turned out to be incorrect. He did not contest his seat at the next election in September 1964, which the Labour Party won under Harold Wilson. After his success in securing White and Edwards, Tommy Butler got the Metropolitan Police Commissioner Sir Joseph Simpson, to suspend his retirement on his 55th birthday so he could continue to hunt the robbers. This paid off with the arrests of first Wilson, then Reynolds. When asked by a reporter after the sentencing of Reynolds whether that was the end of it, Butler replied that it was not over until Biggs was caught. In 1969 he was finally forced to accept compulsory retirement, and later died in 1970, aged 57 years. That same day, Biggs' memoirs were published in The Sun newspaper. Butler's deputy, Frank Williams, was passed over to be his replacement as head of the Flying Squad because of his deal with Edwards ,which he thought would seal his promotion, and his deal with another of the robbers who was never caught. Following this, he left the force to become head of security for QUANTAS airline. He wrote his autobiography *No Fixed Address*, which was published in 1973.

Jack Slipper of the Metropolitan Police was promoted to Detective Chief Superintendent. He became so involved in the case that he continued to hunt many of the escaped robbers after he retired. He believed Biggs should not be released after returning to the UK in 2001 and he often appeared in the media to comment on any news item connected with the robbery before his death on 24 August 2005 at the age of 81.

Detective Chief Superintendent Ernest Malcolm Fewtrell, Head of the Buckinghamshire Crime Investigation Department (CID) was born on 29 September 1909 and died on 28 November 2005, aged 96 years. He retired on the last day of the trial after the verdicts were handed down at the then compulsory retirement age of 55. This allowed him (with Ronald Payne of The Sunday Telegraph, who was involved in the paper's coverage of the case) to be the first of the investigators to write a book *The Train Robbers* on the robbery investigation in 1964. In the book he expressed some frustration with the Flying Squad although he mostly had praise for individual officers. His one regret was that he had the search for the hideout carried out radiating outwards from the scene of the robbery rather than an inwards search from a 30-mile (48 km) perimeter. He worked as an Accommodation Officer for Portsmouth Polytechnic before retiring to live by the sea near Swanage. He continued to express disgust at any film that he felt glamorized the robbers. Fewtrell was assisted and later succeeded in the investigation by John Woolley, who served in the Buckinghamshire Constabulary from 1959 to 1984.

George Hatherill 1898–1986, had his service extended by one year because of the need to complete the investigation of the Great Train Robbery. He visited Canada and the USA as a lecturer on police matters. He died on 17 June 1986 at the age of 87. Gerald MacArthur died aged 70 years on 21 July 1996. He was famous for breaking up the Richardson Gang at a time when a significant number of London-based detectives were known to be corrupt.

One of the Post Office carriages that was part of the remaining train, not involved in the actual robbery, is preserved at the Nene Valley railway at Peterborough, Cambridgeshire, and has been restored. The actual carriage that was robbed, M30204M, was retained for 7 years following the robbery, and then taken to Norfolk and burned in the presence of Police and Post Office representatives at a scrap yard near Norwich in 1970. This was to deter collector/souvenir hunters. Locomotive English Electric type 4-D326 later 40126 was involved in a number of serious operating incidents. The locomotive was scrapped at Doncaster Railway workshops in 1984. The retrieved Monopoly board used by the robbers at their Leatherslade Farm hideout and a genuine £5 note from the robbery is on display at the Thames Valley museum in Sulhamstead, Berkshire. The scene of the crime was for some years called "Train Robbers' bridge" on a Network Rail maintenance sign. This led to an outcry advocating restoration of the original name of Bridego Bridge, but in late 2013 it was renamed again, as Mentmore Bridge. A diorama of the scene has been built by a local club and is currently on display near Aberdeen, at the Grampian Transport Museum.

£2,631,684 was stolen, although the police report says that £2,595,997 was stolen. The bulk of the haul was in £1 notes and £5 notes both the older white note and the newer blue note which was half its size. The £5 notes were bundled in batches of £2,500, the £1 notes in batches of £500. There were also ten-shilling notes in batches of £250. A quantity of Irish and Scottish money was also stolen. With the exception of a few 'drinks' for associates, the loot was split into 17 equal shares of around £150,000 each. George Hatherill claims that there were 18 shares. With a few notable exceptions, the money was quickly laundered or divided by friends, family and associates of the robbers. Much was laundered through bookmakers Wilson and Wisbey were themselves bookmakers although, astonishingly, only a few hundred pounds were identifiable by serial number so the robbers could have spent the money without fear of being traced. There were 1,579 notes whose serial numbers were known and the rest of the money was completely untraceable. Although within six months of the robbery ten of the robbers had been locked up awaiting trial and three others were wanted criminals on the run, very little of the money had actually been recovered. This has caused speculation that there was a great deal of robbery loot still out there. In fact, the money was soon seized and spent by predatory gangsters and greedy associates, relatives and lawyers. So the proceeds of the greatest cash robbery in British history were quickly used up, with few of the robbers receiving any real long-term benefit. Less than £400,000 was eventually recovered. Over half of this consisted of the shares of Roger Cordrey £141,017 and Brian Field £100,900. A further £36,000 was recovered from Jimmy White's caravan. Roy James was carrying £12,041 when captured. The final sum recovered was £47,245 that was found in a telephone box in Great Dover Street, Newington, South London. The £47,245 recovered from a telephone box included 57 notes whose serial numbers had been recorded by the bank in Scotland. This money was allegedly part of a deal struck with Frank Williams by 'Alf Thomas'. Piers Paul Read, in *The Train Robbers*, claimed that the police were feeling the pressure because although they had caught many of the robbers, they had failed to recover much of the money. While no evidence had been found against "Thomas", who only had a reputation as a minor thief, some of the identifiable bank notes had been traced back to him through friends who had been charged with receiving. Given that the police had no evidence against 'Thomas', either at Leatherslade Farm or connection with either of the two gangs, Butler was prepared to let him go. Williams convinced Butler to pull 'Thomas' in for questioning and in return for releasing him and not charging his friends with more serious crimes, £50,000 was to be returned. On 3 December 1963, which happened to be the same day that Roy James was taken into custody, the police received an anonymous tip directing them to the money in the phone box. The money was driven up to Aylesbury and taken into custody by Detective Superintendent Fewtrell, who wondered how his London colleagues could know how much money there was. He had to bring in bank clerks to count the damp and musty money to determine the final sum. Williams made no admission to the recovery of the money being the result of a deal with 'Thomas' despite claiming that his negotiations were responsible for the return of this money, Williams in his book *No Fixed Address* (1973) claimed not to know the identity of the person who had returned the money, although he did mention several robbers to whom he had offered deals through intermediaries. He noted that it seemed to him that Butler was sceptical of his efforts and that at the press conference Hatherill and Millen did not reveal the circumstances behind the find and that he was never asked to talk with them about it. Despite 'Alf Thomas' being the man identified as the assailant of the train driver Jack Mills by Bruce Reynolds, Williams only makes mention of the assailant once in his book. In this section (often quoted by other sources), he confirms that, with Tommy Butler, he questioned the man they knew to be the assailant but that they had no evidence to convict him. Strangely, however, he makes no further mention of him. This lends credence to the claim that a deal was done with 'Alf Thomas' which later caused outrage in the police hierarchy. It is hinted in several books that the deals done by Williams were responsible for his being overlooked for promotion and that Williams was unhappy that his efforts were not recognised by Butler, but were instead hidden from superiors. For his part, George Hatherill, in his book *A Detective's Tale*, stated that the motive behind the return of the money was not known for certain. He said that the money was returned by 'one about whom extensive inquiries had been made and who in fact was interrogated at length. But in spite of our strong suspicions, nothing could be proved against him and so no charge could be brought. My belief is that he thought we knew more about him than we did, and thinking things were getting hot, he decided to get rid of the money to avoid being found in possession with it' Hatherill does not mention Williams at all in his book. He retired on the last day of the trial at Aylesbury.

The ten gang members who were arrested shortly after the robbery had to spend a large amount on legal fees it is thought around £30,000 each. Lawyers were aware of the sums involved and their fees rocketed.

The robbers who spent much time on the run overseas Reynolds, Wilson and Edwards, had very little left when finally arrested, having had to spend money avoiding capture and indulging in lavish lifestyles without finding employment. Much of Jimmy White's money was taken from him. According to Marilyn Wisbey, her father's share was hidden by his father Tommy Wisbey Senior in the panels in the doors of his home. Butler raided them three times but he never found the train money. The majority of the money was reputedly entrusted to Wisbey's father and also to his younger brother Ron, who coincidentally had saved some money of his own that was confiscated by the police but was returned to Ron three months later. By the time Wisbey was released from jail all of his share had either been spent or invested. Marilyn agrees with Piers Paul Read's assessment of how her father's share of approximately

£150,000 was spent. Although the Wisbey share was one that was not taken by other criminals, Marilyn Wisbey is still bitter that her relatives got to spend a fair amount of the loot while the overall sum dwindled away. However, her grandfather did use some of the money to buy them a house in Upper Norwood, South London. Three of the robbers escaped punishment in one way or another the '*Ulsterman*', John Daly who was lucky to have his charges dismissed at the trial and Ronnie Biggs who escaped from jail and managed to avoid being taken back to the UK. John Daly had entrusted his money to another crook. This man had betrayed him to the police and had absconded with the money. He died before Daly could catch up with him. Upon the release of the others in the mid-1970s, Bill Jennings got in touch with Buster Edwards and Frank Monroe got in touch with the South Coast Raiders. Both said that they had no money left. Alf Thomas had disappeared and John Daly at the time was said to be living on the dole in West Country. Ronnie Biggs quickly spent his share getting a new life abroad in Australia, although by the time his family arrived in 1966, all but £7,000 had been spent. £55,000 had been paid as a package deal to get him out of the UK. The rest had gone on legal fees and expenses.

****

CHAPTER 12
BRUCE REYNOLDS

Bruce Richard Reynolds (7 September 1931 – 28 February 2013 was an English criminal who masterminded the 1963 Great Train Robbery. At the time it was Britain's largest robbery, netting £2,631,684 equivalent to £60 million today. Reynolds spent five years on the run before being sentenced to 25 years in 1969. He was released in 1978. He wrote three books and performed with the band Alabama 3, for whom his son, Nick, plays. They wrote the Sopranos theme.

Bruce Richard Reynolds was born at Charing Cross Hospital, in the Strand, central London, the only child of Thomas Richard and Dorothy Margaret (née Keen). He was initially brought up in Putney, and his mother, a nurse, died in 1935 when he was aged four. His father, a trade-union activist at the Ford Dagenham assembly plant, married again, and the family moved to Gants Hill. Reynolds found it difficult to live with his father and stepmother, choosing often to stay with one or other of his grandmothers. During the London Blitz of the Second World War he was evacuated to Suffolk and then to Warwickshire. On leaving school at 14½, Reynolds failed the eyesight test to join the Royal Navy, and decided he wanted to become a foreign correspondent, so he applied in person for a job at Northcliffe House. Employed first as a messenger boy, he then worked in the accounts department of the Daily Mail. By the age of 17 he had become bored with the routine and was working in the Bland/Sutton Institute of Pathology at Middlesex Hospital, before joining Claud Butler as a bicycle messenger and a member of their semi- professional racing team, where he first met criminals and began a life of crime.

After undertaking some petty crime and spending time in HMP Wormwood Scrubs and Borstal for theft, he spent six weeks of the required two years doing National Service in the British Army, before running away to return to petty crime. Sentenced to three years in 1952 for breaking and entering, he was sent to the juvenile wing of Wandsworth Prison in London. He then graduated to jewellery theft from large country houses. In 1957 Reynolds was arrested, together with Terry Hogan, for assault and robbery of a bookmaker returning from White City Greyhounds with £500. The police stated their belief that the intent of the cosh attack was grievous bodily harm and not robbery. Hogan was sentenced to 2½ years and Reynolds received a year longer. After spending time in HMP Wandsworth and HMP Durham, on release in 1960 he then became an antiques dealer and thief. He joined a gang with future best friend Harry Booth and future brother-in-law John Daly. Later on, he did some work with Jimmy White and met Buster Edwards at one of Charlie Richardson's South London clubs. Richardson in turn introduced him to Gordon Goody. Having gained the nick name Napoleon because of his careful planning of robberies, in 1962 his gang stole £62,000 in a security van robbery at London Heathrow Airport. They then attempted to rob a Royal Mail train at Swindon, which netted only £700. But Reynolds, now looking for his career-criminal defining moment, started planning his next train robbery over a period of three months.

Reynolds organised a gang of 15 men to undertake the 1963 Great Train Robbery which he later referred to as his signature heist. After the theft, Reynolds spent six months in a mews house in South Kensington waiting for a false passport. He then travelled via Elstree Airfield to Ostend, was then driven to Brussels Airport, before flying with Sabena airlines to Mexico City via Toronto. Assuming the name Keith Clement Miller, he was joined by his wife Frances, who changed her name to Angela, and son Nick. He later said that at that time in his career 'I was beginning to see the thief as an artist … Nothing could match the tension, excitement and sense of fulfilment.' For Christmas 1964, the family were joined in Acapulco by fellow train robbers Buster Edwards, who had not yet been caught, and treasurer Charlie Wilson, who had escaped from HMP Winson Green. Reynolds and his family later moved to Montreal, Quebec, Canada, where Wilson had settled with his family, but a proposed theft of Canadian dollars was stopped due to Royal Canadian Mounted Police observation. Reynolds then moved to Vancouver, before returning that summer to the South of France. By now running low on cash, he heard a similarly sized large robbery was being planned. The family returned to London, before then moving to Torquay, Devon. Assuming the name Keith Hiller, the family began a life of settling into Reynolds' former childhood holiday town, before he had the urge to make contact with his old friends back in London. The Metropolitan Police whilst watching the London criminal scene realised that Hiller was in fact Reynolds, and arrested him in Torquay on 9 November 1968. He was offered a deal by the Director of Public Prosecutions to plead guilty and avoid them pursuing his son, wife and family on further criminal charges, Reynolds agreed to plead guilty and was sentenced to 25 years. All of the Great Train robbers were held in maximum security in a specially built unit at HMP Durham. He renewed his friendship with both Charlie and Eddie Richardson whilst in prison, Reynolds was released from HMP Maidstone in 1978 and after a failed attempt in the textile trade, he began trafficking and money laundering for many South London drugs gangs. Arrested for dealing amphetamines, he was jailed in the 1980s for three years.

On release he gained a profile in the media and acted as a consultant on the film Buster, with Larry Lamb portraying Reynolds. Reynolds then published his autobiography The Autobiography of a Thief (1995). In the book Reynolds commented that the Great Train Robbery had proved a curse that followed him around, as after it no-one wanted to employ him either legally or illegally 'I became an old crook living on handouts from other old crooks.' Having either spent or had removed by courts the monies that he gained through crime, by the 1990s Reynolds was living on income support in a flat in Croydon, Greater London, supplied by a charitable trust. Reynold's wife predeceased him. He died on the afternoon of 28 February 2013 at the age of 81. His grave is in Highgate Cemetery and forms part of some 'Crime Tours'.

****

CHAPTER 13
THE KRAYS

Twin brothers Ronald 'Ronnie' Kray (24 October 1933 – 17 March 1995) and Reginald 'Reggie' Kray (24 October 1933 – 1 October 2000) were English gangsters who were the foremost perpetrators of organized crime in the East End of London during the 1950s and 1960s. With their gang, the Firm, the Krays were involved in armed robberies, arson, protection rackets, assaults, and the murders of Jack 'the Hat' McVitie and George Cornell.

As West End nightclub owners, they mixed with politicians and prominent entertainers such as Diana Dors, Frank Sinatra, and Judy Garland. They were arrested on 9 May 1968 and convicted in 1969, by the efforts of detectives led by Detective Superintendent Leonard 'Nipper' Read. Both were sentenced to life imprisonment. Ronnie remained in Broadmoor Hospital until his death on 17 March 1995. Reggie was released from prison on compassionate grounds in August 2000, eight weeks before his death from cancer.

The passage of time has turned these two violent men into Robin Hood types in their domain. Nothing could be farther from the truth. In present day law they would both have been sectioned early in their criminal careers and Ronnie would probably have faced pedophilia charges.

Ronnie and Reggie Kray were born on 24 October 1933 in Hoxton, East London, to Charles David Kray (10 March 1907 – 8 March 1983), a scrap gold dealer, and Violet Annie Lee (5 August 1909 – 4 August 1982). They were identical twins, Reggie being born 10 minutes before Ronnie. Their parents already had a seven-year-old son, Charles James (9 July 1927 – 4 April 2000). A sister, Violet (born 1929), died in infancy. Ronnie almost died in 1942 from a head injury suffered in a fight with Reggie. The twins first attended Wood Close School in Brick Lane, and then Daniel Street School. In 1938, the Kray family moved from Stean Street in Hoxton, to 178 Vallance Road in Bethnal Green. At the beginning of World War 2, their elder brother 32-year- old Charles Kray was conscripted into the army, but he refused to go and went into hiding.

The influence of their maternal grandfather , Jimmy 'Cannonball' Lee, a bare knuckle fighter, caused the brothers to take up amateur boxing, then a popular pastime for working-class boys in the

East End. Sibling rivalry spurred them on, and both achieved some success. They are said never to have lost a match before turning professional at age 19.   The Krays were notorious locally for their gang and its violence, and narrowly avoided being sent to prison several times. Young men were conscripted for National service at this time, and in 1952 the twins were called up to serve with the Royal Fusiliers. They reported, but attempted to leave after only a few minutes. The corporal in charge tried to stop them, but Ronnie punched him on the chin, leaving him seriously injured. They walked back to the East End and the next morning they were arrested and turned over to the army. Their behaviour in army prison was so bad that they both received dishonourable discharges. During their few weeks in prison, when their conviction was certain, they tried to dominate the exercise area outside their one-man cells. They threw tantrums, emptied their latrine bucket over a sergeant, dumped a large food/liquid container full of hot tea on another guard, handcuffed a guard to their prison bars with a pair of stolen cuffs, and set their bedding on fire. When they were moved to a communal cell, they assaulted their guard with a china vase and escaped. Quickly recaptured and awaiting transfer to civilian authority for crimes committed while at large, they spent their last night in Canterbury drinking cider, eating crisps, and smoking cigarillos courtesy of the young national servicemen acting as their guards. Their criminal records and dishonourable discharges ended their boxing careers with promoters refusing to have anything to do with them, and so the brothers turned to crime full-time. They bought a run-down snooker club in Bethnal Green, where they started several protection rackets. By the end of the 1950s, the Krays were working for Jay Murray a criminal from Liverpool and were involved in hijacking, armed robbery and arson, through which they acquired money to buy and take other clubs and properties. In 1960 Ronnie Kray was imprisoned for 18 months for running a protection racket and related threats. While he was in prison, Peter Rachman, head of a violent landlord operation, gave Reggie a nightclub called Esmeralda's Barn on the Knightsbridge end of Wilton Place in exchange for protection and debt collecting services. The location is where the Berkeley Hotel now stands.

        This increased the Krays' influence in the West End, by

now making them celebrities as well as criminals. They were assisted by a banker named Alan Cooper, who wanted protection from the Krays' rivals, the Richardsons, based in South London who he had stolen money from. In the 1960s, they were widely seen as prosperous and charming celebrity nightclub owners and were part of the swinging London scene. A large part of their fame was due to their non-criminal activities as popular figures on the celebrity circuit, being photographed by David Bailey on more than one occasion and socializing with Lords, MPs, socialites and show business characters including actors George Raft, Judy Garland, Diana Dors, Barbara Windsor and singer Frank Sinatra. 'They were the best years of our lives. They called them the swinging sixties. The Beatles and The Rolling Stones were rulers of pop music, Carnaby Street ruled the fashion world… and me and my brother ruled London. We were fucking untouchable…' So said Ronnie Kray.

The Krays also came into the public attention when an exposé in the Sunday Mirror alleging that Ron had had a sexual relationship with Lord Boothby, a Conservative politician made headlines. Although no names were printed, after the twins physically threatened the journalists involved and Boothby threatened to sue, the newspaper backed down. It sacked the editor, printed an apology and paid Boothby £40,000 in an out-of-court settlement. Because of this, other newspapers were unwilling to expose the Krays' connections and criminal activities. Much later, C4 established the truth of the allegations and released a documentary on the subject, *The Gangster and the PervertPeer* (2009).

The police investigated the Krays on several occasions, but the brothers' reputation for violence made witnesses afraid to testify. There was also a problem for both main political parties.The Conservative Party was unwilling to press the police to end the Krays' power for fear the Boothby connection would again be publicised, and the Labour Party's MP Tom Driberg was rumoured to have had a relationship with Ron Kray as well.

When Inspector Leonard "Nipper" Read of Scotland Yard was promoted to the Murder Squad, his first assignment was to bring down the Kray twins. It was not his first involvement with them.

During the first half of 1964, Read had been investigating their activities, but publicity and official denials of allegations of Ron's relationship with Boothby made the evidence he collected useless. Read went after the twins with renewed activity in 1967, but frequently came up against the East End "wall of silence", which discouraged anyone from providing information to the police on fear of physical violence to them or their family and their house being torched. Nevertheless, by the end of 1967 Read had built up enough evidence against the Krays to proceed. Witness statements incriminated them, as did other evidence, but none made a convincing case on any one charge. Early in 1968 the Krays employed a man named Alan Bruce Cooper, who sent Paul Elvey to Glasgow to buy explosives for a car bomb. Elvey was the radio engineer who put Radio Sutch, later renamed Radio City, on the air in 1964. Police detained him in Scotland and he confessed to being involved in three murder attempts for the Krays. The evidence was weakened by Cooper, who claimed he was an undercover agent for the United States Treasury Department investigating links between the American Mafia and the Kray gang. Read tried using Cooper, who was also being employed as a source by one of Read's superior officers, as a trap for the Krays, but they avoided him having been tipped off. Eventually, a Scotland Yard conference decided to arrest the Krays on the evidence already collected in the hope that other witnesses would be forthcoming once the Krays were in custody. On 8 May 1968, they and 15 other members of their 'firm' were arrested. Many witnesses came forward now that their reign of intimidation was over, and it was relatively easy to gain a conviction. The Krays and 14 others were convicted, with one member of the Firm being acquitted. One of the firm members who provided a lot of the information to the police was arrested yet only for a short period. The twins' defence, under their counsel John Platt-Mills QC, consisted of flat denials of all charges and the discrediting of witnesses by pointing out their criminal past. The judge, Mr Justice Melford Stevenson said 'In my view, society has earned a rest from your activities.' Both were sentenced to life imprisonment, with a non-parole period of 30 years for the murders of Cornell and McVitie, the longest sentences ever passed at the Old Bailey for murder. Their brother Charlie was imprisoned for 10 years for his part in the murders. On

11th August 1982, under tight security, Ronnie and Reggie Kray were allowed to attend the funeral of their mother Violet, who had died of cancer the week before, but they were not allowed to attend the graveside service at Chingford Mount Cemetery in East London where their mother was interred in the Kray family plot. The service was attended by celebrities including Diana Dors and underworld figures known to the Krays. The twins did not ask to attend their father's funeral when he died in March 1983, to avoid the publicity that had surrounded their mother's funeral.

In 1985, officials at Broadmoor Hospital discovered a business card of Ron's, which prompted an investigation. It revealed the twins – incarcerated at separate institutions, plus their older brother Charlie and an accomplice not in prison were operating a lucrative bodyguard and protection business for Hollywood stars visiting the UK. Documents released under Freedom of Information laws revealed that officials were concerned about this operation, called Krayleigh Enterprises, but believed there was no legal basis to shut it down. Documentation of the investigation showed that Frank Sinatra hired 18 bodyguards from Krayleigh Enterprises during 1985. At the time Sinatra was represented by the mob and the Kary's old mentor Bert Rossi who had handled the mob's London business had probably recommended them.

Ronnie Kray was a Category A prisoner, denied almost all liberties, and not allowed to mix with other prisoners. Reggie Kray was locked up in Maidstone Prison for 8 years as Category B. In his later years, he was downgraded to Category C and transferred to Wayland Prison in Norfolk.

Ronnie was eventually certified insane in 1979 and lived the remainder of his life in Broadmoor Hospital in Crowthorne, Berkshire. He died on 17 March 1995 of a heart attack, aged 61, at Wexham Park Hospital in Slough, Berkshire.

During his incarceration, Reggie became a born again Christian. After serving more than the recommended 30 years he was sentenced to in March 1969, he was freed from Wayland on 26th August 2000. He was almost 67, and was released on compassionate grounds for having inoperable bladder cancer. The final weeks of his life were spent with his wife Roberta, whom he had married whilst in Maidstone Prison in July 1997, in a suite at the Townhouse Hotel in Norwich, having left Norwich Hospital on 22nd September 2000. On 1 October 2000, Reggie died in his sleep. Ten days later, he was buried beside his brother Ronnie in Chingford Mount Cemetery.

Older brother Charlie Kray was released from prison in 1975 after serving seven years, but was sentenced again in 1997 for conspiracy to smuggle cocaine in an undercover drugs sting. He died in prison of natural causes on 4 April 2000, aged 73.

Ronnie was openly bisexual, evidenced by his book *My Story* and a confession to writer Robin McGibbon on *The Kray Tapes*, wherein he states: 'I'm bisexual, not gay, bisexual.' He also planned on marrying a woman named Monica in the 1960s whom he had dated for nearly three years. He called her 'the most beautiful woman he had ever seen.' This is mentioned in Reggie's book *Born Fighter*. Also, extracts are mentioned in Ron's own book *My Story* and Kate Kray's books *Sorted, Murder, Madness and Marriage*, and *Free at Last*. Ron was arrested before he had the chance to marry Monica and, even though she married Ronnie's ex-boyfriend, 59 letters sent to her between May and December 1968 when he was imprisoned show Ron still had feelings for her. He referred to her as 'my little angel' and 'my little doll'. She also still had feelings for Ronnie. The letters were auctioned in 2010. A letter, sent from prison in 1968, from Ron to his mother Violet also mentions Monica; 'if they let me see Monica and put me with Reg, I could not ask for more.' He went on to say, with spelling mistakes, 'Monica is the only girl I have liked in my life. She is a luvely little person as you know. When you see her, tell her I am in luve with her more than ever.' Ron subsequently married twice, wedding Elaine Mildener in 1985 at Broadmoor chapel before the couple divorced in 1989, following which he married Kate Howard, who he divorced in 1994. In 1997 Reggie married Roberta Jones. In an interview with author John Pearson, Ronnie indicated a strong identification with Gordon of Khartoum and accepted as true an unproved theory about him 'Gordon was like me, homosexual, and he met his death like a man. When it's time for me to go, I hope I do the same.' There was a long-running campaign, with some minor celebrity support, to have the twins released from prison, but successive Home

Secretaries vetoed the idea, largely on the grounds that both Krays' prison records were marred by violence toward other inmates. The campaign gathered momentum after the release of a film based on their lives called The Krays in 1990. Produced by Ray Burdis, it starred Spandau Ballet brothers Martin and Gary Kemp, who played the roles of Reggie and Ronnie respectively. Ronnie, Reggie and Charlie Kray received £255,000 between them for the film. Reggie wrote 'I seem to have walked a double path most of my life. Perhaps an extra step in one of those directions might have seen me celebrated rather than notorious.' Others point to Reggie's violent prison record when he was being detained separately from Ronnie and argue that in reality, the twins' temperaments were little different. Reggie's marriage to Frances Shea in 1965 lasted eight months and she left although the marriage was never formally dissolved and died 2 years later in suspicious circumstances. An inquest came to the conclusion that she committed suicide, but in 2002 an ex-lover of Reggie Kray's came forward to allege that Frances was actually murdered by a jealous Ronnie. Bradley Allardyce who spent 3 years in Maidstone Prison with Reggie explained, 'I was sitting in my cell with Reg and it was one of those nights where we turned the lights down low and put some nice music on and sometimes he would reminisce. He would get really deep and open up to me. He suddenly broke down and said, 'I'm going to tell you something I've only ever told two people and something I've carried around with. He put his head on my shoulder and told me Ronnie killed Frances. He told Reggie what he had done two days after. A British television documentary, *The Gangster and the Pervert Peer* 2009, showed that Ronnie Kray was a man-on-man rapist commonly referred to in criminal circles as a 'nonce'. The program also detailed his relationship with Tory peer Boothby as well as an ongoing *DailyMirror* investigation into Lord Boothby's dealings with the Kray brothers.

The Valence Road house was demolished to make way for a housing estate much to the sadness of the many 'Kray pilgrims' who used to visit and photograph it but their graves at Chingford Mount Cemetery are still a regular stop on the 'Kray Tour' and usually covered with flowers on the anniversaries of their deaths.

Ronnie Kray shot and killed George Cornell, an associate

of the Richardsons, leaders of a South London gang, at the Blind Beggar public house in Whitechapel on 9 March 1966. Ronnie was drinking in another pub when he learned of Cornell's location. He went there with his brother's driver John Dickson and his assistant Ian Barrie but killed Cornell alone. Just before he died, Cornell remarked, 'Well, look who's here.' There are differing motives offered for the murder. Cornell's position as a leader of an opposing gang that was threatening the Krays and that he had previously insulted Ronnie Kray. Cornell was thought to have a part in the murder of Ronnie's former associate, Richard Hart. Ronnie Kray was already suffering from paranoid schizophenia at the time of the killing. According to some sources, Ronnie killed Cornell because on Christmas 1965, during a confrontation between the Krays and the Richardson gang at the Astor Club, Cornell referred to Ronnie as a 'fat poof'. The confrontation resulted in a gang war, and about three months later, on 8th March 1966, Richard Hart, Ronnie's associate, was murdered at 'Mr Smith's Club' in Catford. A member of the Richardson gang 'Mad' Frankie Fraser was taken to court for Hart's murder but was found not guilty. Another member of the Richardson gang, Ray Cullinane testified that he saw Cornell kicking Hart. Due to intimidation, witnesses would not cooperate with the police in Hart's case, and the trial ended inconclusively without pointing to any suspect in particular. Cornell was the only one to escape the brawl at Mr Smith's Club without major injuries, and was probably suspected by Ronnie as having an important role in Hart's murder. But, at court, Ronnie denied that he had been insulted and that the murder was in order to avenge Hart's death. Instead, he claimed that the reason for the murder was because Cornell had been threatening the Kray brothers.

The Krays' criminal activities continued to be hidden behind their celebrity status and legitimate businesses. In October 1967, four months after the suicide of his wife Frances, Reggie was alleged to have been encouraged by his brother to kill Jack 'the Hat' McVitie, (see his own section later in the book) a minor member of the Kray gang who had failed to fulfil a £1,500 contract paid to him in advance to kill Leslie Payne. McVitie was lured to a basement flat in Evering Road, Stoke Newington owned by 'Blonde' Carol a call girl living with a gang member at the time, on the pretence of a party. As he entered, he saw Ronnie Kray seated in the front room and as Ronnie approached him he gave him a load of verbal abuse and as the argument got more heated Reggie Kray pointed a handgun at McVitie's head and pulled the trigger twice, but the gun failed to discharge and McVitie was held in a bearhug and Reggie Kray was handed a carving knife. He stabbed McVitie in the face and stomach, driving it deep into his neck, twisting the blade, and continuing to stab as McVitie lay on the floor dying although it was thought that Reggie never originally intended to kill McVitie and he was only lured to the basement flat to be put straight by the twins about fights he had caused in their protected clubs, but not killed. Several other members of the Firm including the Lambrianou brothers,Tony and Chris, were convicted of this. In Tony Lambrianou's biography, he claims that when Reggie was stabbing McVitie, his liver came out and he had to flush it down the toilet. McVitie's body has never been recovered although it was rumoured that it was taken through the Blackwall tunnel rolled in a carpet and dumped over a church wall. When Ronnie Kray was told that he phoned Freddie Foreman on whose 'turf' the church was and Foreman retrieved the body and took it to an Essex pig farm where it was cut up and devoured by the animals. Others say it was weighed down, wrapped in chicken wire and dumped at sea. Who knows? Freddie Foreman does but will he tell? Not so far.

Frank Samuel Mitchell (see his own section later in the book) 1929 – 24th December 1966, also known as 'The Mad Axeman', was an English criminal and friend of the Kray Twins who was later murdered at their behest. Mitchell was one of seven children born into a working-class family from Limehouse, East London. At the age of nine he stole a bicycle from another child for which he was taken before a juvenile court and put on probation. As an adult, Mitchell possessed great physical strength and liked to demonstrate it by lifting a grand piano off the floor or picking up two fully-grown men, one in each hand. He also had a short temper and, according to psychiatrists who treated him the mind of a child of 13 or under. From the age of 17 Mitchell was regularly incarcerated in borstals and prisons, mostly for shop-breaking and larceny. During a brief spell of freedom, he fathered a daughter with a girlfriend, but he never knew about her. In prison Mitchell was total pain in the ass. His prison terms were characterised by violence against guards and fellow inmates, and he was punished with the birch and the cat-o-nine tails. He was one of the ringleaders in a riot at Rochester Borstal. He slashed a guard across the face, and was charged with attempted murder after attacking an inmate he believed had informed on him. He was later acquitted. In 1955 he was diagnosed 'mentally defective' and sent to the Rampton psychiatric hospital. Two years later Mitchell escaped with another inmate, and they attacked a man with an iron bar before stealing his clothes and money. When he was recaptured Mitchell attacked police with two meat cleavers, and was again sent to Broadmoor. He escaped again, broke into a private home and held a married couple hostage with an axe, for where came his nickname 'The Mad Axeman' in the media. In October 1958 he was sentenced to life imprisonment for robbery with violence. Mitchell was sent to Dartmoor Prison in 1962, and whilst there his behaviour improved. He kept budgerigars and was transferred to the honour party, a small group of trusties who were allowed to work outside the prison walls with minimal supervision. Mitchell was permitted to roam the moors and feed the wild ponies and even visit nearby pubs. On one occasion he caught a taxi to Okehampton to buy a budgerigar. The governor of the prison promised Mitchell that if he stayed out of trouble he would recommend to the Home Office that he be given a release date. Four years later, Mitchell was aggrieved that he had still not received one. Mitchell had befriended Ronnie Kray when they served a sentence together at Wandsworth Prison in the 1950s. During Mitchell's trial for attempted murder, Ron hired a lawyer for him and paid for him to have a new suit fitted. Ron was keen on breaking Mitchell out of Dartmoor prison, thinking it would help him to publicise his own grievance and earn a release date for Mitchell, as well as enhance the Krays' standing in the underworld. Reggie Kray recalled that he was reluctant, but finally reasoned that 'if nothing else it would stick two fingers up to the law'. Reggie visited Mitchell at Dartmoor in disguise and informed him of the plan. On 12 December 1966, while with a small work party on the moors, Mitchell asked the sole guard for permission to feed some nearby ponies. His request was granted, he walked over to a quiet road where a getaway car containing associates of the Krays – Albert Donoghue, Teddy Smith and Billy Exley were waiting for him, and drove him to London where the Krays put him up in a flat in Barking Road, East Ham. It was over five hours before Mitchell was reported missing at Dartmoor. Mitchell's escape made national news, led to a political storm over the lax security around a man described in the press as 'Britain's most violent convict', and was debated in the House of Commons. A large manhunt ensued, with 200 policemen, 100 Royal Marines and a RAF helicopter searching the moors. With the aid of Teddy Smith, Mitchell wrote to the national newspapers and his plea to be granted a release date was printed in The Times and the Daily Mirror. However, Home Secretary Roy Jenkins was not willing to negotiate with an escaped felon and would not review his status until he was back in custody. Mitchell soon became a big problem for the Krays. Owing to his physical strength and short temper, he was difficult to control. He was unwilling to give himself up and return to prison, and was not allowed to leave the flat in East Ham in case he was recognised. The Krays could not release him from the flat or turn him in to the police as he could implicate them in his escape. Mitchell felt insulted that Reggie had only visited him in person once at the flat and was particularly upset that he could not visit his parents, despite them living nearby. He grew increasingly agitated and began making threats against the Krays. To placate him, they brought a woman to the flat, Liza Prescott, a blonde night club hostess, with whom Mitchell soon fell in love, further complicating the situation. The Krays decided the only solution was to kill him. On 24th December 1966, Christmas Eve, Mitchell was led into the back of a van by Albert Donoghue thinking he was to be taken to a safe house in the countryside where he would meet up with Ronnie Kray and work things out. There was almost another argument when he realised that Liza would not be coming with him but Donoghue persuaded him that it was safer for her to follow later on. Waiting in the van were several men, among them Freddie Foreman and Alfie Gerrard, who were armed with revolvers. Once the van doors were closed and the engine started, they opened fire on Mitchell, killing him. Donoghue thought that 12 shots were fired before Mitchell died. His body was never recovered. Foreman later revealed that Mitchell's body was bound with chicken wire, weighted down and dumped in the English Channel. Reg Kray cited springing Mitchell from prison as one of his biggest mistakes and wished he had never done it. In 1968, the Krays and various accomplices were arrested and put on trial for an array of offences, including the murders of George Cornell, Jack McVitie and Frank Mitchell. Their attempt to cajole gang member Albert Donoghue into confessing to killing Mitchell alone annoyed Donoghue and led to him becoming a crown witness and testifying against them. Ronnie, Reggie and Charlie Kray along with Freddie Foreman were all acquitted of Mitchell's murder due to lack of evidence and the perceived unreliability of Donoghue's testimony. Reggie Kray was found guilty of conspiring to effect Mitchell's escape from Dartmoor, for which he received a five-year sentence to run concurrently with his other sentences. Donoghue and another Firm member, John Dickson, pleaded guilty to harbouring Mitchell and respectively received 18-month and nine-month sentences. In his 1996 autobiography *Respect*, Foreman admitted to shooting Mitchell as a favour to the Krays. Donoghue said Foreman was paid £1,000 for it. Foreman was arrested and questioned by police after repeating his confession in a 2000 television documentary, but the CPS announced that it would not be re-opening the case, due to the then extant double jeopardy law, since rescinded so they could have another go at him now but it is highly unlikely seeing Foreman's age.

****

CHAPTER 14
THE LAMBIANOU BROTHERS

Chris and Tony Lambrianou were brothers from an upright family in North West London. Their father was Greek and their mother Irish. Both being hardworking parents and making a go of their restaurant business. The boys were two of five children and as far as we know were the only ones that drifted into a criminal career.

From early youth sentences in jail for theft they moved into bigger crime and came to the attention of Freddie Foreman and the Krays. The Krays way of working was that they didn't actually commit any crimes themselves and always had others do the deed or they took a percentage from the take of any robberies on their East London turf. If you were in with the Krays then you were protected and over time the Lambianous got in with the Krays.

Seeing a limit to what they could achieve criminally in London because of this unspoken rule that you had to clear it with the Krays first, the brothers moved out and up to the West Midlands and Manchester where they got involved setting up 'long firm' scams by building up a business over a year or so, usually in the drinks, luxury goods or cigarette trade and gradually gaining confidence of the suppliers who they paid straight away until whallop! A big order was placed for Xmas stock or similar and the firm and the stock disappeared overnight. They also were involved in Club life and criminal partnerships which included Charlie Kray who was running clubs in the Midlands at the time. The brothers were soon established as the top team in that area.

Their biggest regret must be their friendship, albeit a means to an end, with the Krays as it was the murder of Jack McVitie that was their undoing. The brothers were in London and out drinking with mates when Tony suggested they go on to the Regency Club, a club protected by the Krays and a well known hang out for villains. It was a place to avoid on a Saturday night as young 'wannabees' would often cause a fight with better known 'faces' to try to impress. But Tony insisted they go and as soon as they got inside Jack McVitie came over and joined them as did the Mills brothers. When Tony was getting a round of drinks McVitie told Chris that he didn't trust Tony who he thought was too far 'in' with the Krays. He was going to be proved so right with that. When Tony came back with the drinks he said there was a party at 'blond Carols' place down the road. Blond Carol was call girl who flitted from one criminal boyfriend to the next and just part of the scene as were so many 'ladies of the night'. There was no party at Blond Carol's place 65 Evering Road, McVitie, the Mills and the Lambrianous were greeted by Ronnie Hart a member of the Kray Firm who led them down to the basement where a trap had been laid for Mcvitie who had become a thorn in the side of the Krays by causing too much trouble in their 'protected' pubs and clubs because of his liking for beer and violence. The Krays had already warned him about it and told him to behave himself in their 'protected' premises but he had mouthed off about them being weak and a 'pair of puffs'. And that couldn't be allowed. When they all entered the basement at Blond Carol's there was no party, no girls just the Krays and immediately Reggie Kray put a gun to McVitie's head and pulled the trigger. It failed to fire, twice. Chris Lambrianou quickly left the building shouting over his shoulder that he wanted 'nothing to do with this stuff.'

Outside he was caught up by Connie Whitehead and then the Krays and half a dozen of their minders who were in the building came out too. Ronnie Kray asked 'What's the matter with Chris?' Connie Whitehead told Ronnie, 'He didn't know this was going to happen. 'Ronnie said, 'Take him home.' So Whitehead took him home to the Lambianou family flat in Queensbridge Road. But after a while to calm down Chris realised that his brother Tony was part of this plan to kill McVitie otherwise why had he been so insistent on going to the Regency Club where McVitie was known to hang out a lot and then for all of them to go to the 'party' that didn't exist. He went back to Blond Carol's and found Ronnie Bender a small time Kray 'hanger-on' and driver the only one there. He said everyone had gone and left him to get rid of the body.

'What body? Asked Chris. 'McVitie's' replied Bender.

At that point brother Tony turned up and they all went to the basement where McVitie's body lay in the middle of a pool of blood on the floor where Reggie Kray had stabbed him many, many times.

Blond Carol arrived home with her current boyfriend and they were told to go upstairs to the flat and forget what they'd seen. She later became a key Prosecution witness against the Krays and the Lambianous in the Old Bailey. More on that later. The body was wrapped in an old eiderdown and the room cleaned before pulling McVitie's own car up outside the house and putting him in the boot. The first idea was to chuck the body onto a railway line where the next train would mash it to an unrecognisable pulp and the police would think a drunk McVitie had wandered onto the line in a drink filled stupor. But the nearest line was difficult to get to so the next idea was to take the body to South of the River and dump it on the Richardson's manor so they would be prime suspects. Just through Rotherhithe tunnel they lost their nerve and dumped the car and its contents by St Mary's Church and all went home.

The Lambrianou brothers fled to Birmingham and were surprised that there was nothing in the papers or on the news about the McVitie murder until they learnt a few days later that the Krays had been made aware of what had happened to the body, probably by Bender, on the same night it was dumped and they didn't want it to be found on another firm's turf as that would lead to war and anyway they had good relations with Freddie Foreman who's manor that was and wanted to keep it that way. You clear up your own mess was an unwritten code and you do not move it onto another manor. So it is alleged that they got Freddie Foreman and his Deptford team to get the body and dispose of it for a fat fee. Unsubstantiated rumour has it that McVitie ended up as pig food on an Essex pig farm.

At this time a team of Scotland Yard detectives under Commander John du Rose had been given the order by the Home Secretary to bring down the Krays as they were becoming too popular and too big. The only way this would be done was by persuading somebody close to them to grass them up. And that is exactly what happened. On October 28th 1967 Nipper Read arrested the Krays and most of the others who were at the party and in his interview with Chris Lambianou Read told him exactly what had happened at Blond Carol's and Lambrianou realized that could only have come from somebody who was there and had struck a deal with the Police so knew their fate was sealed.

It was both Blond Carol and Ronnie Hart who stood up in court at the trial and told the whole story. The Lambianous defence that they didn't see anything and were not even there was blown to smithereens. If Chris Lambianou had told the police the truth that he was outside the room and not physically involved in what had happened he would have probably got a short sentence but for some reason he kept saying he wasn't there and the Police had witnesses who said he was. So he was implicated in the murder by a false sense of loyalty to the Krays which had put him in the frame when he had no need to be in it at all. He had thought that had he admitted to being there then he would have been made to testify against the Krays and confirm they were there. They had denied being present as well. The jury returned verdicts of guilty of murder on all of them. Reggie Kray got life; Ronnie got life; Ian Barrie a Kray hard man got life with 20yrs recommendation; Tony Lambrianou got minimum 15 years, Chris Lambianou got life with minimum 15 years and the other players all got lesser sentences.

In later years Chris 'found' God, got married and had twins although he divorced later. He lives in Oxfordshire as at 2021. Tony died in 2004.

****

CHAPTER 15
THE RICHARDSONS

Charlie Richardson 18th January 1934 – 19th September 2012 was born in Camberwell, South London. His younger brother, Eddie, was born in January 1936, followed by youngest sibling, Alan (born 1940). Charlie and Eddie turned to a life of crime after their father deserted the family who lived first at Wren Road in Camberwell where his granny had a sweetshop and his mum helped out, they then moved to a flat in Wyndham Road when the Second World War broke out. Later they moved to Champion Hill living a few doors down from Freddie Mills the boxer who was found dead outside his Charing Cross Road nightclub in 1965, and then when Eddie got married he moved out and to Sidcup. When they were older Eddie and Charlie would hang around boxing clubs like the Fitzroy club on the Walworth road or go to the Locarno, later named The Cat's Whiskers in Streatham. Eddie bought a scrap yard in Camberwell called KWP Metals when he was released after his first stretch in prison, there was nowhere in South London the Richardson's didn't label as their patch.

The Richardson Gang was also known as the 'Torture Gang', they had a reputation as being London's most sadistic gangsters. Their alleged specialities included pulling teeth using pliers, cutting off toes using bolt cutters, and nailing victims to the floor using 6-inch nails all of which Eddie said in later interviews were just 'fairy tales'. Charlie invested in scrap metal, whilst Eddie operated fruit machines. These businesses were fronts for underworld activities which included fraud, racketeering, usury, theft and fencing stolen goods. Eddie would on occasion 'suggest' that a pub landlord should buy one of his slot machines, failure to do so meant running the risk of having the pub vandalised every evening until the machine was installed. Charlie was at one point arrested for receiving stolen goods, but was acquitted through lack of evidence and, allegedly, with the help of a large 'donation' to the Police Fund. The brothers preferred investing in fraud schemes known as long firms. A company would be set up by an acquaintance who was well paid for the prison term he would eventually serve. The company would conduct normal business for some months, building lines of credit and winning the trust of suppliers. Eventually they would place a very large order on credit; the goods would then be sold for cash, the money pocketed, and the company and those involved in running it would suddenly disappear. Later on the

Richardson's ran a string of clubs from the Cavern in Lordship Lane, Dulwich, to the Orange Club in Walworth Road and The Shirley Anne in New Cross. The clubs were stocked with stolen booze and stolen cigarettes for the most part. Profits were high. At the peak of their empire they were a formidable force with henchmen like "mad" Frankie Fraser only too willing to do their bidding. 'Today, I would not like to meet the likes of me as I was then' says Richardson in his autobiography, The Last Word: My Life As A Gangland Boss.

An important member of the Richardson gang was George Cornell. Cornell was heavily involved in drug dealing 'purple hearts' and 'dexys' known as 'uppers and 'downers' plus cannabis. He was also involved in pornography and may have been associated with Jimmy Humphreys, who was responsible for the exposure of corrupt police officials in 1971, including Commander Ken Drury of the Flying Squad. Humphreys was under investigation by another squad, and Drury refused to acknowledge his association with Humphreys even after Drury reportedly received a 'Wish you were here' holiday postcard from him. Cornell was originally a member of an East End gang called 'The Watney Streeters' and later became involved with the Krays. However, he changed sides around 1964 and allied himself with the Richardsons. Cornell was unstable, unpredictable and nearly caused an all-out war between the two gangs before his shooting and death in 1966.

'Mad' Frankie Fraser teamed up with the Richardson gang in the mid-1960s. His criminal career began at age 13 with theft. During World War 2 his crimes escalated, including shop breaking and desertion. He was a known associate of gangster Billy Hill throughout the 1950s. After joining the Richardsons, he served as their enforcer. Reportedly, Fraser's favourite brand of punishment was extracting teeth with pliers. Over his long criminal career, Fraser spent 42years in prison. He died in 2014 of natural causes.

Other notable characters in the gang included the hitman Jimmy Moody, Roy Hall, Bartholomew (Barry) Harris who sat as the getaway driver for the gang, Albert Longman, Frank Bailey, Tommy Clark and various members of my extended family. The Richardson gang frequently used mock trials to punish transgressors and intimidate others. The accused were hauled in front of Charlie, Fraser and others in a kangaroo court at the scrap yard in Camberwell or one of the clubs. After the mock trial the punishments were given out, anything from beatings to more severe forms of torture: whippings, cigarette burning, teeth being pulled out with pliers , nailing to the floor, having toes removed with bolt cutters and given electric shocks until unconsciousness. The electric shocks were inflicted by an old Army field telephone which included a hand cranked power generator, much like the notorious Tucker Telephone; the terminals were attached to the victims' nipples and genitalia and they were then placed in a bath of cold water to enhance the electrical charge. After trial and punishment, victims who were too badly injured would be sent to a doctor who had been struck off the Medical register and liked cash. This process of trial and torture was known as 'taking a shirt from Charlie', because of Charlie Richardson's habit of giving each victim a clean shirt to return home in since the victim's original shirt was usually covered in blood. On one occasion, a collector of the gang member's *'pensions'*, protection money from publicans and others, was punished after being twice warned by the Richardsons for pocketing the money and spending it at Catford dog track. He was nailed to the floor of a warehouse near Tower Bridge for nearly two days, during which time gang members frequently popped in and urinated on him. In later years, however, Frankie Fraser claimed that the charges of torture were exaggerated. He cried 'rubbish' to stories of electrified genitals. In reference to the allegations of foot-nailing and tooth removals, he said 'all false… today, we wouldn't have even been charged, let alone gone to prison.'

FEUD WITH THE KRAYS

The Richardson gang and the Kray Twins were engaged in a turf war in the mid- to late 1960s. Charlie Richardson and George Cornell had first met the Krays while serving time in Shepton Mallet Prison. Tensions came to a head during a Christmas party at the Astor Club in December 1965, Cornell called Ronnie Kray a 'Fat Poof' and a fight ensued. On 7 or 8 March 1966, Richard Hart, one of the Krays' associates, was shot dead, intentionally or otherwise, during a brawl at Mr Smith's Club in Rushey Green, Catford. Mr Smith's was owned by Manchester-based businessmen Dougie Flood, a club/hotel/leisure business owner and alleged member of the Manchester's Quality Street

Gang and Bill Benny. They had asked Eddie Richardson and Frankie Fraser to 'protect' the club in exchange for gaming machines being placed there. On the night in question, both groups were 'drinking and chatting quite happily' according to a guest who was with his girlfriend in the bar but who was suddenly ushered out of the club soon after midnight. Around 1 a.m., Eddie Richardson told Peter Hennessey a Kray Firm member and the others to 'drink up' and leave. In response, Hennessey called Eddie Richardson a 'half-baked fucking ponce' and shouted that he could 'take you any fucking time you like.' Richardson and Hennessey began exchanging blows, other fistfights started and shots rang out. Several years after the incident, an unnamed gangster who was in the club at the time, said that it was 'like Dodge City'. It was said that Hart was shot on or near the bottom of the stairs as he was making his getaway. For many years, Fraser was held responsible for shooting Hart, although he always vehemently denied it. It is alleged that Billy Gardner confronted Fraser, asking 'are you tooled up, Frank?', and shot Fraser through the thigh with a .38 pistol. Eddie Richardson, Frankie Fraser and others ended up in Lewisham Hospital and denied all knowledge of the incident asking the police who came to interview them, 'Shooting? What shooting?' Hennessey sustained a bayonet wound to his scalp. Hennessey, Gardner and others sought help from Freddie Foreman down the road at Greenwich after the altercation and, although most of the gang were arrested, some were put up by Foreman until things had blown over. Although Fraser was declared insane at least twice previously it has been suggested that Fraser acquired his 'Mad' nickname from this incident. Apparently Henry Botton, a Hayward associate, saw Fraser kicking Hart in the head and shouted 'You're fucking mad, Frank. You're fucking bonkers.' Fallout continued the next day. A member of the Richardson gang, Jimmy Andrews, was injured in the affray and went for treatment in the Whitechapel Hospital the day after. This was where George Cornell, an old friend of his, went to visit him and became very upset at the extent of his mate's injuries. That evening Cornell was seen walking down Whitechapel Road, drunk or drugged, shouting 'Where's that fat wanker?' referring to Ronnie Kray. At about 8.30pm, he went into The Blind Beggar public house and started shouting insults about the Krays. Ronnie Kray arrived with two associates and shot Cornell through the head at close range. One of several locals in the saloon bar at the time, claimed he heard Cornell's last words which were 'Well, look what the dog's brought in.'One old gentlemen who was in the pub at the time and asked to be a witness by the police said 'I'd rather not, I don't like the sight of blood, especially my own.'

The downfall of the Richardsons came about because of the highly public nature of the Mr Smith's Club affair and because of mounting testimony told to the police. In July 1965 one of the gang's victims had had enough and reported the crime to the police. The victim told the tale of being severely beaten and bruised after being found guilty of disloyalty by a Richardson kangaroo court and then had to mop up his own blood using his own underpants. Another member of the Richardson gang, Johnny Bradbury, turned Queens Evidence. Bradbury was convicted of murdering a business associate named Waldeck in South Africa, allegedly on orders from Charlie Richardson who had mining interests out there. When sentenced to hang, Bradbury offered to inform on the Richardson gang in exchange for a pardon and immunity. This was arranged by a special squad of the CID, led by Inspector Gerald MacArthur. Word of this soon got round and other victims of the Richardsons were granted immunity from prosecution in other crimes if they turned Queen's Evidence. With the assistance of the Home Office, who arranged different identities and passports, several witnesses fled the country immediately after the trial. A few went to South Africa and others to Spain or Mallorca; many did not return to the UK for a considerable time if at all.

Charlie Richardson was arrested for torture on 30th July 1966, the World Cup Final day. Eddie Richardson was sent to prison for 5 years for affray. There were also stories of Charlie being connected to the South African Bureau of State Security and an attempt to tap the Prime Minister's telephone. In July 1966 police arrested the remaining members of the gang following a series of raids in South London. The so-called Torture Trial convened at the Old Bailey at the beginning of April 1967. The Richardsons were found guilty of fraud, extortion, assault and grievous bodily harm. Charlie Richardson was sentenced to 25 years in prison, and Eddie had 10 years added to his existing sentence. Charlie Richardson was not freed until July 1984.

In 1980, after many attempts to obtain release, Charlie

Richardson escaped from an open prison. He went 'on the trot' for almost a year, even dressing as Santa Claus and giving out presents to children to publicise his requests for release. He openly drank with friends and old associates including police officers at several pubs on the Old Kent Road before fleeing to Paris, where he gave interviews to journalists. He was arrested with five other men in Earls Court on suspicion of possession of drugs, having just been seen coming out of a sex shop which was known to be controlled by the Richardson family. His identity only came to light once arrested and in police custody at Kensington when his probation officer contacted the police having been informed by other gang members that he had been arrested. In 1983, Charlie was able to go on day release to help the handicapped and was allowed to spend a weekend with his family. Charlie was finally released in July 1984. In 1990, Eddie Richardson was back in court and sentenced to 35 years after being convicted of involvement in a £70m cocaine and cannabis heist. He was originally sentenced to 35 years, but was released after 12, bringing his total number of years served to 23. The brothers fell out badly after Eddie accused Charlie of fraudulent business deals during Eddie's time in prison.

Charlie Richardson died of peritonitis in September 2012. A heavy smoker, he had suffered from emphysema for several years.

Their 'manor' stretched from South London scrap yards and West End clubs to mining interests in South Africa and their empire was said to have embraced fraud, gambling and protection rackets. Both skipped National Service, Charlie by cutting up his uniform and pretending to be mad. The pair then proceeded to build their empire. It was partly legal, through scrap metal and foreign investments and mostly illegal, through frauds, protection rackets and clubs. While they lorded over South London, their main gang rivals were the Kray twins, Ronnie and Reggie, in the East End. There was no love lost between the two gangs as the Mr Smith Club fracas showed. Eddie called the Krays 'brainless of Britain'.

'You had the Krays and the Richardsons around at the same time, but I think the Richardsons were more violent than the Krays,' former Detective Superintendent John Cummings has said. 'The Richardsons were frighteners, really vicious people and the Krays decided not to take them on for the South London 'manor', a very good decision.'

Charlie was officially released in 1984 and later became a campaigner for young offenders.

In the 90s to the present day (2021) Eddie he lives in a £2.5 million house in Beckenham, Kent, drives a big, fat silver Mercedes, holidays in Marbella, organises charity golf competitions and paints pricey portraits of friends and, occasionally, their dogs 'so much easier than people'.

He also hires himself out for 'nostalgia lunch dates' £300 for a slap-up fish and chip lunch and a chat. There are the Kray brothers he says, 'both gay and both brainless of Britain. In prison Reggie used to get The Times every day, but never once opened it'. And Frankie Fraser 'Game for anything you asked him'. Not forgetting the Great Train Robbers 'really nice men', the prison reformer Lord Longford 'always scruffy but he never rammed religion down your throat' and Brian Keenan, then head of the armed council of the IRA 'lovely fellow but not brilliant at bridge'. But Eddie's favourite subject, other than his autobiography, 'it's so good some people have read it 20 times' was prison. Which isn't surprising given he's spent over a third of his life behind bars as a Double Category 'A' prisoner. 'That's one step up from Category 'A',' he says with pride. 'You have to have two screws with you everywhere you go. They were scared of me. I was always working out how to crack the system.' Which he did and soon boasted an array of special privileges that included his own TV, constant access to the prison yard and a steady stream of epicurean delights and post prandial brandies. 'A few of us took turns to cook for ourselves, I once did a Christmas dinner for 16 with a 20lb turkey and I always had an after-dinner brandy. In one prison we had so much food, legs of lamb, joints of beef, chickens, so much that we couldn't get it all in the prison fridge. I had to apply to the governor for permission to buy another fridge.' Permission was granted.

He was also involved in a prison mutiny, a six-week hunger strike, countless assaults and a failed escape attempt which left two guards in hospital. 'We were supposed to be making a nice wooden cabinet in the woodwork class, but actually made two 26ft ladders and no one noticed.' Eleven years later, including an extra 450 days for bad behaviour, Eddie returned home to his scrap metal business, all his old friends and, funnily enough, sufficient funds to pay for a glamorous life skiing, bobsleighing and jet-setting around the world. But it was only a matter of time before he was caught out again. Cash flow slowed down and the £70 million cocaine and cannabis heist caught his eye.

'I used to turn down loads, but this one looked too good. I knew the people this end, I knew the South Americans. I thought I could trust them. If we'd got away with it, we'd have made a lot of money. But c'est la vie we didn't.' Instead, he got 35 years eventually commuted to 13, bringing his total served years to 26.

Under DCS MacArthur's leadership, the Hertfordshire Police force were the investigating force that put the case together and arrested the Richardsons because the Home Office could not trust the Metropolitan Police, many of whom were known to be in the pay of the Richardsons and other London gangs. By 1966, the Metropolitan Police was allegedly so corrupt that the then Home Secretary, Roy Jenkins, was considering replacing up to 70% of the CID and other specialist branches with CID from Manchester, Kent, Devon & Cornwall and Birmingham. When Robert Mark became Police Commissioner in 1972 he succeeded Sir John Waldron. More than 400 CID officers and 300 uniformed police officers were "retired" early. Not long after Mark's appointment, Drury, Wally Virgo, Head of the Serious Crimes Squad, and other senior officers were sent to prison for corruption.

****

CHAPTER 16

1971 BAKER STREET ROBBERY
& PRINCESS MARGARET PHOTOS.

On September 1st 1971 after taking almost three months to tunnel under a branch of Lloyds Bank in Baker Street, three robbers forced open more than 260 safety deposit boxes and walked away with more than £3million (more than £45m today).

In Wimpole Street, London, amateur CB radio enthusiast Robert Rowlands is tuning his set at around 1am. trying to tune in to popular European station Radio Luxembourg. Radio Luxembourg doesn't come through his speakers, Rowlands had unwittingly picked up walkie- talkies operating on ordinary public frequencies and the conversation is between criminals and about a bank robbery in progress. But which bank and where? Once Rowlands heard enough to know what he'd stumbled on he called the police. The officer he spoke to, given that it was 1am. on a Saturday morning, assumed it was yet another hoaxer who'd taken one drink too many and politely suggested that if Rowlands heard any more suspicious chatter he should record it and ended the call.

Rowlands then recorded every time the unknown crooks started talking and dialed the police a second time. This time he was absolutely insistent that a major robbery was still in progress and this time Scotland Yard detectives were sent to his home to talk it through and listen to the tape. What they heard caused a major alert and search operation. It was clear from the tape that a major robbery was still in progress and, if they moved quickly enough they stood a good chance of finding exactly which bank was being robbed and of catching the robbers red-handed.

What followed was a successful heist, a huge score for the robbers, a serious blunder by Scotland Yard, stiff sentences for the robbers and a crime that lent a seemingly baseless conspiracy aspect to the 2008 feature film THE BANK JOB. The film alleges that it was masterminded by the British Security Service MI5 to recover compromising photographs of senior public figures including Princess Margaret which were being used by a London criminal to blackmail authorities into letting him continue operating. The entertainment business decided to take a perfectly good story and add fictional, often unnecessary spice to it, that's been happening for decades when criminals and heists are involved. But, like so many films based on real events, the Baker Street Robbery never really needed spicing up in the first place.

Like most criminal enterprises it was, theoretically at least, simple. Thieves targeted a branch of Lloyds Bank, one of Britain's best- known banks, intending to break into the safety-deposit vault, force open as many deposit boxes as possible in the time available and escape with whatever they found worth taking. Safe-deposit vaults are sometimes considered a tempting target for robbery because, as a rule, only high-value items such as jewellery, bearer bonds, securities, uncut gems and large amounts of cash tend to be kept in them and, once robbers breach the vault, whatever they find is likely to be worth the time, effort and expense of breaking in. Bank robbers in the UK had never taken such a huge haul before the Baker Street robbery and none have managed it since except perhaps the Hatton Garden heist. The theory was simple, the practice wasn't. To reach the vault the robbers had to choose a nearby empty shop which they had an accomplice rent, break through the floor to a depth of 5 feet, tunnel 40 feet under the Chicken Inn fast food shop between their shop and the bank itself, then tunnel 15 feet back up (owing to sloping ground), break through three feet of reinforced concrete forming the vault floor, break open hundreds of deposit boxes, sort through them for anything worth taking and then escape back through the tunnel with the loot. All this had to be done without tripping any of the vault's security devices or arousing any public attention while digging the tunnel and robbing the vault. To succeed the plan needed time, patience, significant funding, technical expertise with explosives and a thermic lance needed to breach the concrete floor and no small amount of luck. Such a robbery, on such a scale, was simply unheard-of in the UK in 1971. Given the technical difficulties and obvious physical risks it's not hard to see why. The gang chose to tunnel under the vault because the walls and ceiling were steel plated and protected by vibration alarms and trembler switches that would sense unusual vibrations or shockwaves and automatically trigger an alarm direct to the police. The vault door was protected by a similar alarm that would be triggered by the door either being opened or directly attacked. Through a contact at the local security company protecting the bank the gang knew that the tremblers in the vault floor were turned off at that time due to false alarms caused by road works nearby, a major security lapse. A safecracker will often ignore a safe door and try forcing either the base, sides, top or back of an ordinary safe because the door is usually the strongest, best- protected part of it. Bank vaults can often be attacked along similar lines, albeit on a larger scale. Police estimated that the gang took almost three months to lease the nearest available ground-floor property which was a leather goods store named Le Sac just two doors down from the bank, assemble the equipment, dig the tunnel, breach the vault floor and steal its contents. It was a highly specialised robbery needing considerable technical expertise which makes it unusual that the gang themselves weren't high-level experts as much as journeyman crooks making an unusually complex entry into the big leagues.

The Baker Street robbery involved four principal players, none of whom had a record or reputation for the higher leagues of crime. Desmond Wolfe leased the store used as the tunnel entrance which was something that would come back to bite him later on. Anthony Gavin, Thomas Stephens and Reginald Tucker did the tunnelling and the robbery itself. All these men were known to the police, but none was thought to have the skills for something as complex and difficult as this. Police suspected but were never able to prove that the crime was actually masterminded by another London criminal whose identity was never established and the robbers themselves never gave anything to the police to confirm those suspicions. The gang only dug at weekends, minimizing the risk of anyone noticing unusual noise which explained the time taken to dig the tunnel. The debris and rubble were stored inside the leased shop which had its windows painted white and a sign placed on the door stating that it was closed for refurbishment. To any passing pedestrian or policeman on his beat it was just another empty store and the noise inside would easily be put down to the interior being reshaped before re-opening under new management. Having tunnelled under the Chicken Inn between their shop and the bank they were faced with another obstacle, three feet of reinforced concrete floor between them and the inside of the vault. They originally chose a thermic lance known as a burn bar to cut through the vault floor, but eventually had to blow a hole using explosives. The burn bar was taking too long and creating dense, toxic fumes in the tunnel itself making it impossible for the robbers to finish the job that way. Having burnt through half the floor and blasted the rest of the way but leaving enough depth of concrete to avoid bank staff noticing any cracks or putting their feet through the weakened section they were in position to wait to make their final move. In 1971 British banks were usually closed from Friday afternoons until Monday mornings, giving the robbers the maximum time between burgling the vault and the crime being discovered when the bank re-opened. All they had left to do was break through the remaining concrete floor, enter the vault and break into as many deposit boxes as possible overnight. Or so they thought, anyway. The robbers were smart enough to keep one of their number as a look-out on a nearby rooftop and stay in touch via walkie-talkies. The walkie-talkies operated on the Citizen's Band public frequencies where anyone could intercept the conversations and listen in. The likelihood of their chatter being intercepted was fairly small and not something they had taken into consideration. At that time amateur radio enthusiasts were growing in numbers, CB radios were still technically illegal to use in 1971 and expensive to buy, few people had them and so it's unlikely the gang thought about whether they were providing a commentary to their robbery for anybody who accidentally or otherwise found the right frequency. Robert Rowlands did. The chase was now on to figure out the gang's exact location and hopefully catch them in the act. It didn't quite work out as Scotland Yard, would have liked.

Having had to make not one phone call, but two before the police would send officers to visit him, Rowlands made a point of telling the police that the range of walkie-talkies at the time was quite short, especially in urban areas with tall buildings. He told the officers that if his ordinary set was picking up walkie-talkie chatter then that meant the robbers and their target couldn't be more than a mile or two from his Wimpole Street flat. Baker Street is within two miles of Wimpole Street. If it had been acted on Rowlands's information about the radio's range would certainly have narrowed the search area significantly, making it far more likely that the gang would have been caught red handed. But it wasn't acted on. The gang escaped from the crime scene taking over £3,000,000 of assorted swag that would be worth around £45,000,000 at current values. Instead of using Rowlands's radio knowledge to concentrate the search the police decided to visit every bank within 10 miles of his home, some 750 in all, and check all of them as quickly as possible. Given the gang's use of CB radios police also tried mobilizing radio detection vehicles from the Post Office. Prior to privatizing national utilities during the 1980's, pinpointing unlicensed radio transmissions came under Post Office jurisdiction. Unfortunately, like the banks, the Post Office worked conventional hours as well and didn't have any detection vehicle crews on duty at 1a.m. on a Saturday morning. The police, aside from the sheer number of banks they had to check, could only enter private property without a warrant when there was cause to believe a crime was actually in progress inside that property. In order to work through the list of possible targets the police would have to contact and transport the managers of all the banks listed so they could open their premises and check their vaults, an impossible logistic task. The police couldn't simply force entry to any private address ie a bank, on the off-chance of raiding the right one, all they could do was check the premises for signs of forced entry and listen for any noise. Fred Karno's Army springs to mind! All this took time to arrange. Enough time for the robbers to drill through the last inches of the vault floor, enter the vault, open over 260 deposit boxes, rifle their contents and escape with whatever loot they wanted. It wasn't until the Monday morning that the manager of the Baker Street branch of Lloyds, which was one that had been checked without anything unusual being spotted, entered the bank, opened the safe-deposit vault and was greeted by piles of discarded high-value property, hundreds of smashed deposit boxes and a man-sized hole in the middle of the floor. What the manager said isn't on record, but he immediately called the police. Scotland Yard was faced with considerable public embarrassment. Investigators also now had a vast amount of evidence to sift through even before they could start to identify and catch the gang responsible for what was at the time the biggest robbery in British criminal history.

The amount of evidence was huge and time was short, London's banking community and over 260 less-than-happy customers were in a state of shock. The owners of every box forced open had to be identified, informed and asked exactly what they had deposited which, for any depositor with anything either highly embarrassing or outright illegal in their box, could have caused serious problems and many refused to tell.

Every one of the hundreds of pieces of loot left behind had to be catalogued and photographed, the tunnel had to be made safe to enter before being traced back to its source, evidence left in the tunnel and the leather goods store had to be catalogued and examined and then the police could actually start hunting for the gang themselves. They needed every lucky break they could get and, for the first time in the case, they actually got one. It was a small break but it proved to be absolutely vital. Desmond Wolfe was in the leather goods trade when not breaking the law and it was Wolfe who leased the shop the gang used as a base. Unfortunately for him and the rest of the gang Wolfe provided lasting proof of his not being a criminal genius not the brightest tool in the box by leasing it under his own name. It wasn't long before Wolfe was safely under lock and key being asked to answer a few questions. With one gang member under arrest, the police looked for Wolfe's known criminal associates, especially those who didn't have alibis, had a criminal record for burglaries and similar crimes and weren't already in jail for unrelated offences. Soon, Anthony Gavin, Thomas Stephens and Reginald Tucker were all under arrest and being questioned by Scotland Yard detectives. True to the criminal code, none of the four men offered any information or offered to give evidence in return for lighter sentences when the case came to trial. In January 1973 all four men were convicted. Wolfe received only eight years due to his age, he was 64 at the time, while Gavin, Stephens and Tucker all received stiff penalties of 12 years each.

Two other men were tried for allegedly handling stolen money from the robbery and were acquitted. Not a single item of stolen property from the Baker Street robbery has ever been recovered, not one.

There have always been unanswered questions about this robbery. First, it was highly unusual for relatively low-level criminals to tackle something needing such special skills and equipment. Using a thermic lance isn't for novices and whoever set the explosives managed to blow a hole in the vault floor without setting off any of the other security devices protecting the vault itself. That suggests a higher level of technical skill than the gang members themselves were known to have. This raised the possibility that there were others involved who managed to evade detection even today. The sheer scale of the tunnel is also far bigger and more complex than any job any of the robbers had tackled before, suggesting either an unusual degree of criminal ambition or that perhaps more outside help than they ever admitted to. Not one of them cracked under questioning, none of them cut a deal in return for lighter sentences and, so far, none of them has opted for a book deal or made any public comment about either the crime or the fact that none of the swag has ever been found. So somebody somewhere may have had far more luck and made far more money than anybody involved in the actual robbery itself.

As far as can be confirmed, the 2008 film 'The Bank Job' which poses a theory about MI5 setting up the robbery to recover blackmail material is a theory and nothing more. The story goes that a London criminal known as "Michael X" real name Michael de Freitas and originally from Trinidad possessed incriminating photographs of Princess Margaret taken on her favourite holiday island of Mustique, and De Freitas used the threat to publish them to force Scotland Yard to turn a blind eye to his long-term criminal operations involving the London 'Yardies'. Having been forced to leave London when police attention became too serious on The Yardies he resurfaced in Trinidad where he was later tried, convicted and hanged for ordering a local murder. The film's makers suggest that the robbery deprived him of his lifeline against prosecution, the photos, thus forcing him to leave Britain before being arrested. The suggestion is that there was a media blackout after the robbery. There was not. The police *did* impose a blackout while the robbery was in progress, hoping to catch the gang red-handed, but once the gang had committed the crime and escaped with the loot there was no need or point in continuing it. Rowlands states he was told a so-called D Notice was issued to suppress the story which, again, is extremely unlikely. What was then known as a D Notice (Defence Notice) could be issued by a government department concerned with preserving national security by advising the press to avoid discussing certain matters such as intelligence operations or the current activities of Special Forces troops. A D Notice however was and still is not legally enforceable in itself, amounting only to the government advising the media to keep something quiet. Then as now the press is not obliged to obey one even when its modern-day equivalent the Defence Advisory Notice is issued. Secondly, there are no official records logging any request for a D Notice nor for one having been issued for this case and there certainly would be records if it had been issued. Michael X was a professional criminal, a slum landlord, pimp and sometime enforcer. If MI5 was so desperate to see him silenced to suppress the publication of the Margaret photos then a relatively simple 'gangland' killing would have been easier to arrange. There's nothing especially unusual about gangland feuds and related violence in London at that time, so just another dead mid-level gangster is unlikely to have caused either much comment or any unwelcome curiosity.

To sum up, the Baker Street robbery was an unusual moment in British crime, but not nearly as unusual as some people might believe or others might like them to. At the time it was one of the largest robberies in British history, the method was highly unusual and the gang members themselves not the type of robbers anybody expected to tackle something so complex. There's also a question mark over whether or not a Mr. Big actually put the job together, whether or not all those involved were actually caught and where all the stolen cash and property finally ended up. Somebody must have arranged its onward sale and disposal of the proceeds, but nobody was ever convicted for having done so and although the police kept a sharp on the known 'fences' of this quality jewellery none was seen to handle it. But the evidence supporting the suggestion that this was really arranged by some shadowy spymasters at MI5 to protect the high and mighty entirely unconfirmed. There's almost nothing to suggest that this was a conspiracy cooked up in the corridors of power, but there's plenty to suggest that, while it was a huge score and very difficult to pull off, it was simply another case of a gang of crooks robbing a bank because, to quote legendary New York bandit Willie Sutton, 'King of the Bank Robbers' 'That's where the money is.'

****

CHAPTER 17

1983 The curse of Brink's Mat

It was Saturday, November 26 1983, and what followed on that chilly morning still reverberates today.

It was pitch black and icy cold when security guard Richard Holliday arrived to open Unit 7 on a scruffy trading estate near Heathrow Airport. Inside this nondescript warehouse was one of Britain's biggest secure vaults, used to store currency, precious metals and other high-value consignments. Four colleagues joined him, but the fifth man rostered for duty that day, 31-year-old Tony Black, was late and when he finally showed up he looked pale, unkempt and worried. After a short while Black disappeared, mumbling something about having a bad curry the night before and needing the toilet, but instead he went to the front door, where his brother-in-law Brian Robinson and fellow robbers   Mickey McAvoy, Brian Perry and three other men were armed and waiting in a stolen blue Transit van. Thanks to Black, the robbers knew the vault contained gold, cash and jewellery worth up to £3 million.

They even knew which of the two security guards had the combination numbers for the safes inside.

.   The Brink's-Mat bullion theft remains the biggest and most notorious heist ever to take place in the UK. Worth a staggering £520 million at today's gold prices, the robbery transformed not just Britain's criminal underworld but the face of Britain itself, its financial tentacles helping to unleash a tide of illegal drugs into the country and with it the accompanying gang violence. The double-strength Ecstasy that killed schoolgirl Leah Betts in 1995 was almost certainly brought into Britain using some of the Brink's Mat proceeds. The consequences have also been devastating for the gangsters who took part in *the crime of the century*. Brink's Mat gold robbery has claimed more than 20 lives so far, with countless more ruined. Some have been shot dead as a warning to the rest of the underworld, others disappeared without trace. And there is no sign that the killings are going to stop. Only one third of the bullion has been recovered and the case remains open. Even today, a new generation of British, Romanian and Albanian gangsters based in London are locked in a vicious battle for the remaining ingots which, they believe, now lie secreted in the lock-ups of South-East London or under the fields of Kent. 'One by one those originally involved have been being picked off like targets in a funfair shooting gallery,' says one of the police detectives involved in the original investigation. It is known in the underworld as The Brinks Mat Curse.

The first the security guards inside Unit 7 making a welcome hot pot of tea knew of the raid after Banks had let the gang in was when a man in a yellow balaclava pointed a semi-automatic pistol at their faces and told them all to hit the floor. Believing it to be a colleague playing a practical joke, Peter Bentley laughed and continued to make the tea. Without a word, the gunman coshed him with the Browning Automatic and he fell to the floor. The guards were cuffed and bound at the shins with heavy-duty duct tape. Cloth bags with strings were then pulled down over their heads. The two security men who held the combinations were soon identified and separated from the others. One of them had his trousers pulled down and petrol poured in his lap. He was warned a match would be lit and a bullet put in his head if he didn't give out the proper vault combination. Terrified, the two were frog marched to the vault door and told to enter the combinations and open it. One guard punched in his half of the combination to the vault before his colleague was pushed forward to complete the sequence. Only after 20 terrifying minutes of fear with a gun at his head did he get the code right.

It was shortly before 7am when the gang finally stepped inside the vault, where fluorescent lights revealed a carpet of drab grey containers, no bigger than shoeboxes. Inside each container were 12 perfectly formed bars of pure gold. The robbers were not expecting this and prized off a few more lids to reveal the same awesome sight. There were a total of 6,800 gold bars, weighing three-and-a-half tons and worth £26,369,778. They also found hundreds of thousands of pounds, travellers cheques and rough diamonds – it was an Aladdin's cave of treasure. The atmosphere was electric as the gang hurriedly began passing bars of gold to their battered Transit van reversed up to the door. It was not long before the vehicles axles were bending under the weight. More than one eyewitness later reported seeing an old van with a wheezing engine riding very low on its suspension through the streets of Hounslow. None of the gang had experience with gold. There was far too much for their usual 'fences' in the Birmingham and London jewellery trade to handle so it was not surprising, as the word spread across the underworld, that various top London villains, or 'faces', let it be known that they would be pitching for the 'rights' to turn all that gold into ready cash. 'The robbery was the simple bit,' one criminal said. 'Now the real fun begins.'

The police soon made the connection between Tony Black, the 'inside man' and Robinson, his brother-in-law. Eight days later, Black admitted his involvement and fingered three of the gang, Robinson, McAvoy and another South-London hood called Tony White. The sheer size of the haul of gold bullion had created a huge problem because the gang needed a conduit through which the gold could travel. It had to be smelted, disguised and sold back into the gold industry before it could be turned into cash. The robbers had to look outside their close circle of associates to find people to handle the gold, and here they made a big mistake. Villains who had known each other for years were now having to put their trust in people such as Kent crime boss Kenneth Noye, who had convinced McAvoy and Robinson he was the best man to help them turn the gold into cash. The other main player was a 31-year-old 'businessman' from Bath called John Palmer. He was later dubbed 'Goldfinger' after he was accused and cleared of dishonestly handling gold from the robbery. (see his section later in the book)

At first, Noye was as good as his word. His mob generated a torrent of money for the gang. In the four months following the robbery, one bank handled transactions of more than £10 million, mainly held in grubby plastic bags. But it was while Noye was plotting how to convert yet more of the gold into cash with a South London crook called Brian Reader (see the Hatton Garden Security Vault Robbery) that the Brink's-Mat villains hit their second major setback. By January 1985, Noye, already under suspicion, was being watched by undercover officers, including Detective Constable John Fordham. When Fordham and a colleague moved on to the grounds of Noye's isolated home in West Kingsdown, Kent, dressed in camouflage gear, disaster struck. Noye's dogs started barking and Fordham found himself fighting their knife-wielding owner and Brian Reader who was present at the house but later denied being involved in the fight. Fordham suffered at least ten stab wounds and died two hours later. Brian Reader fled.

After Fordham's death, his colleagues discovered a hugely

significant piece of evidence linking Noye and Reader to the Brink's-Mat robbery. Lying in a shallow gully beside the garage wall, were 11 gold bars wrapped in red-and-white cloth. The same red-and-white material was later discovered in Noye's Ford Granada, and operating instructions for a smelting furnace were also found in Noye's apple store. Officers were astonished to discover that Goldfinger by Shirley Bassey was primed to play on the stereo system whenever anyone walked into Noye's lounge. Initially, robber Mickey McAvoy was cautious but he then made a classic error by leaving his council house in Dulwich, South London and moving into a mansion on the Kent border. He also bought two rottweilers and named them Brink's and Mat. Other gang members were irritated by his 'stupidity and clumsiness'. Eleven days after being arrested Black had turned Queens Evidence, Robinson (his brother in Law), McAvoy and White were arrested and charged with robbery. Black the grass was sentenced to six years' imprisonment with a warning from the judge that 'Never again will you be safe . . . You and your family will forever be fugitives from those you so stupidly and so wickedly helped.' Then, in November 1984, after a month-long trial, McAvoy and Robinson were found guilty of robbery and each sentenced to 25 years' imprisonment. White was found not guilty. Around this time another of the suspected robbers, George 'Georgie Boy' Francis, was shot in his pub by a gunman who escaped on a motorbike. The curse had begun. Francis survived after an operation to remove a 9mm bullet from his shoulder, but the message had been sent loud and clear to all those connected with Brink's-Mat who had not yet been sent to prison. Keep your mouth shut. By this time, police believed that at least half the gold had been smelted and sold back to legitimate dealers, including Johnson Matthey, to whom, ironically, it belonged in the first place. The remaining gold, worth at least £10 million, was, they believed, buried and undiscovered. Detectives eventually traced some of the proceeds of the robbery to the Isle of Man, the Channel Islands, the British Virgin Islands, the Bahamas, Spain and Florida. Increasing amounts continued to be invested in property in the London Docklands redevelopment boom of the mid-Eighties. A portion was even used to buy a former section of Cheltenham Ladies' College, which was then converted into flats that eventually sold for £1.6 million. Brink's-Mat money was poured into property developments on the Costa del Sol. If you have had a gold tooth cap since 1990 it's probably partly if not wholly Brinks-Mat!! Noye and Reader were found not guilty of the murder of DC Fordham and acquitted but five months later both were jailed in 1986 for handling stolen bullion. It was in jail that Noye became convinced that there was a fortune to be made from Ecstasy. The days of armed robberies were numbered. Security vans were now being monitored with radar by the police, and it was now virtually impossible to rob a bank. As a result, drugs were emerging as the main criminal currency. Ecstasy could be sold to teenagers as user-friendly, although its known side effects, including panic attacks and heart problems, soon became evident. Noye and the Brink's-Mat team could smell a real earner with E. It had the potential to give them a return of ten times on the gold bullion money they would invest in it. Moreover, the investigation into Brink's-Mat was progressing, bank accounts and assets were steadily being frozen so the money needed to be 'washed' quickly. Inside Swaleside Prison in Kent, Noye soon spread the word and set up the routes and distribution for an Ecstasy empire. From the late eighties to early nineties, Brink's-Mat cash would deluge Britain with Ecstasy. One of the detectives involved in the Brink's-Mat inquiry explained: 'There is absolutely no doubt that the flood of Ecstasy into Britain started largely because of the Brink's-Mat cash that was floating around.' The Ecstasy tablet that killed 18-year-old Leah Betts after an evening out in Raquel's nightclub in Basildon, Essex in November 1995 had been supplied by a gang controlled by Pat Tate, Noye's associate and 'minder' when the pair were in jail. Leah's friend Stephen Smith had obtained four tablets and gave one to Leah because it was her birthday. Neither had realised the tablets were double-strength.

The gang's paid contacts inside Kent Constabulary and the Metropolitan Police remained invaluable for getting advance notice of raids. This was before the new Commissioner Sir Robert Marks weeded out the 'bent' coppers in the CID, and hundreds took early retirement or were sacked.

While still in prison, Noye was tipped off that, together, the police and the American Drug Enforcement Administration (DEA) were targeting him along with other members of the Brink's-Mat gang. Noye was told that they almost had enough evidence to implicate him in a huge drug deal he was in the throes of completing so Noye pulled out of the deal and a costly six-month investigation was abandoned.

On his release from jail, Pat Tate ran Essex's main Ecstasy supply route after getting financial backing from Noye and other Brink's- Mat gang members. In 1995, Tate was one of three men found shot in a Range Rover in the Essex countryside. They had been lured there by another Brink's-Mat associate to inspect a landing site for aircraft carrying Ecstasy. Obviously somewhere along the way they had double crossed somebody or taken more than they should have or maybe were playing both sides. Interviews with the police and criminals suggest that Tate wasn't averse to horse-trading with the police. Was the Brink's-Mat gang's involvement in the Ecstasy trade one of the 'titbits' that he offered them? The death toll of those linked to the Brink's-Mat robbery continued to climb as the years went on. In 1987 ex-policeman Daniel Morgan was found with an axe embedded in his skull in a South London car park. It was known that he had encountered Noye and his associates. The Brink's-Mat curse even touched on the Great Train Robbery gang of 1963. One of them, Charlie Wilson, found himself in trouble when £3 million of Brink's-Mat investors' money went missing in a drug deal. In April 1990, he paid the price when a young British hood knocked on the front door of his hacienda north of Marbella and shot him and his pet husky dog before coolly riding off down the hill on a yellow bicycle. Over the next three years, four more shootings were connected to the Brink's-Mat raid. Noye was released from prison in the summer of 1994 but in March 2000 was jailed for life for the M25 'road-rage' murder of motorist Stephen Cameron, committed four years earlier. He was released in 2019. From 1994 to 1997, five more gangland deaths were attributed in some way to Brink's-Mat. The murder of a witness in the Noye road-rage case in October 2000 left another bloody mark and told those that needed to be reminded that even in prison some criminals have power. In November 2001, the shooting in broad daylight of Brink's-Mat robber Brian Perry, 63, as he got out of his car in Bermondsey, South-East London, sent another shiver of fear through the underworld. Perry had been murdered right in the heart of his 'home territory'. One source close to the gang said 'Certain people wanted their share of the gold and when it wasn't there waiting for them when they came out, they started getting very upset. 'The cycle of death continued. A few months after Perry's murder, two of his oldest associates were murdered separately near the Kent ports of Chatham and Rochester. Then, on May 14, 2003, Brink's-Mat gang member George Francis, 63, was gunned down at point-blank range as he sat in his car outside the courier business he ran in South-East London. When a bodybuilder, Stephen Marshall 38, confessed to being the 'dismemberer' for the notorious Adams, Clerkenwell, crime family, it became clear that some of the bodies he had disposed of were murdered because of their links to Brink's-Mat. He had originally been arrested after stabbing a former work colleague to death and cutting his body into pieces. When the body was first discovered it led to the case being known as the Jigsaw Murder as pathologists had to fit the body part together piece by piece. Marshall then stunned detectives by alleging that he'd hacked up four other bodies while working for Terry Adams (see the Adams family section) – Adams was one of the men responsible for laundering the Brink's-Mat gold and more recently allegedly financing the Hatton Garden heist.

As one senior detective who worked on and off the Brink's-Mat investigation for more than 20 years commented, 'Nothing really surprises us any more when it comes to Brink's-Mat, these villains were out of control, many of them off their heads on drugs bought with their new-found riches. The trouble was that when that money either ran out, or in the case of some of them, never materialized, there was only one way to respond and that was to kill people to show others that even 25 years after the robbery was committed, if they dared to cross the gang they would still pay for it with their life.'

The Brink's-Mat conversion of gold into cash brought more money into this country than any other gang of criminals in history. And when they spent it, they often helped keep legitimate businesses afloat in the poorer areas of South-East London, as well Spain's Costa del Sol. It was a complex operation involving both money laundering and the melting down of the gold. But there seems little doubt that the money it generated helped the Kent crime boss Noye turn his favourite Mediterranean haven in northern Cyprus into a smaller but much more dangerous version of the Costa del. Money from Brink's-Mat was used not only to set up timeshare resorts and build hotels in Cyprus, but also to help gangsters with links to the robbery to buy mansions on the island. Along a five-mile stretch of the coast between the port of Kyrenia and the town of Lapta, South-East London villains adopted a champagne lifestyle behind the gates of their luxury homes, similar to that once enjoyed by British crooks in southern Spain. Among them was the secluded £2 million villa of Dogan Arif, unofficial leader of the Arif gangland family who terrorised South London with their robbing and drug-trafficking operations in the Eighties. They also played a role in handling much of the Brink's- Mat gold. One of the problems with the gold was that its purity would quickly arouse suspicion if attempts were made to sell it to legitimate traders. That's where Noye and his knowledge of the smelting trade came in. The high-grade ingots were melted down and mixed with copper to disguise the quality. The trick was so successful that the Assay Office in Sheffield even stamped its seal on some of the cleverly doctored gold. A smelter was later found at the home of Bath businessman John Palmer, but he was cleared of any involvement. Palmer, who often wore body armour, was eventually convicted of timeshare fraud and was jailed for eight years. (See the section on him later in the book.)

The best police estimate is that detectives only ever laid their hands on about 30 per cent of the stolen gold. The rest of it has gone up more than two hundred-fold in value since the heist in 1983.There remains a hard core of 250 'premier league' criminals at the top of the British underworld, many of whom are constantly tracked by the National Criminal Intelligence Service (NCIS). This includes at least three members of the Brink's-Mat gang, still active after all these years.

But Brink's-Mat also marked the end of an era in British crime. Robbery was overtaken by far more lucrative, straightforward enterprises such as drugs, arms dealing, racketeering and people smuggling.

DEADLY ROLL CALL
Since the robbery quite a few of the 'firm' have met untimely or

suspicious ends.

JON BRISTOW. Nothing heard of since.

BRIAN PERRY – Brink's-Mat gang associate shot dead in Bermondsey, South London, in 2001. A short distance from where George Francis was killed, cab firm owner Brian Perry was murdered in a similar fashion – shot three times in the back of the head as he walked from his car to his office. Perry was sentenced to nine years in jail in 1992 for his part in melting down the bullion. Two men were tried for his murder in 2006 and acquitted after the case against them fell apart. His murder remains unsolved but rumours abound about the missing millions being at the root of it.

JOHN FORDHAM – Undercover policeman who was stabbed to death in 1985 by Kenneth Noye.

SOLLY NAHOME – Bullion smelter and Hatton Garden jeweler. Solly Nahome was gunned down on the doorstep of his north London home in 1998. Nahome was said to have been involved in the smelting and laundering of the stolen gold. He was a key financial adviser to the feared north London Adams crime family.

KEITH HEDLEY – Money launderer was shot dead by three men on his yacht off Corfu in 1996. A Noye associate suspected of helping him escape justice.

CHARLIE WILSON – Great Train Robber shot at home in Spain in 1990 along with dog. He was murdered in 1990 when he answered the door at his home in Marbella, Spain. The assassin, who escaped on a bicycle, also shot Wilson's dog. The killing was seemingly ordered after £3m of the Brink's-Mat haul was lost after he invested it.

JOHN MARSHALL - Businessman John Marshall was shot dead in his car in 1996. Along with Palmer, Marshall was said to have helped Noye flee the UK after the "road rage" murder of Stephen Cameron, and then been killed to stop police from discovering the link.

GILBERT WYNTER – Enforcer who disappeared in 1998 is believed to be in foundations of the O2 Arena in South East London.

NICK WHITING –. Kent car dealer Nick Whiting vanished, along with a number of vehicles, in June 1990. His corpse was later found on Rainham Marshes, Essex. He had been shot in the head.

PAT TATE – Associate of Noye shot dead with two other men in Rettendon, Essex, in 1995.

STEPHEN CAMERON – Stabbed to death by Kenneth Noye in 1996 road rage incident on the M25.

LEAH BETTS – Died in 1995 aged 18 after taking ecstasy thought to have been imported using Brink's-Mat money.

DONALD URQUHART – Money launderer who was shot by a hitman in West London in 1995. Property investor Donald Urquhart was also involved in plans to launder the Brink's-Mat proceeds. It proved a bad investment and the money was lost. He was shot dead in a central London street, in January 1993.The motorcycle rider who shot him was paid £20,000, a court was later told.

GEORGE FRANCIS – Publican who handled gold, shot in Bermondsey in 2003. Repeatedly shot as he leant into his car through one of its door windows outside the courier firm he ran in Bermondsey, South London, in May 2003.Two men were convicted of the killing – said to have been ordered after Francis failed to repay an "old debt". Allegations that surfaced before the trial suggested he was given £5m in Brink's-Mat proceeds to help launder – but not all of it was repaid.

JOHN MARSHALL – Associate of Noye shot in Sydenham, South London in 1996.

DANNY ROFF – Gangster mown down in Bromley, Kent, in 1997. London criminal Danny Roff was suspected of being a look-out in Wilson's murder. He was shot dead in his car outside his home in south London seven years later.

SIDNEY WINK – ex detective turned gun dealer believed to have supplied the guns for the Brink's-Mat raid committed suicide by shooting himself in 1994. Suspected of supplying the weapon that killed Urquhart as well as the weapons used to carry out the Heathrow robbery itself. When detectives visited his Essex home in August 1994 to question him they found him dead. An inquest heard he had committed suicide by shooting himself in the head.

ALAN DECABRAL – Witness due to give evidence against Noye ended up peppered with bullets in a car park in Ashford, Kent, in 2000.

JOEY WILKINS – Vice king who grassed on Noye died mysteriously in 2007 after an apparent robbery on the Costa del Sol.

ALAN 'TAFFY' HOLMES – Brink's-Mat detective shot himself in 1987.

MICHAEL OLYMBIOUS – Drug dealer ended up dead in 1995.

JOHN PALMER shot 6 times in his garden 2015

****

CHAPTER 18
1983 RONNIE & JOHN KNIGHT
& THE SECURITY EXPRESS ROBBERY

Wednesday, 2 March 1983, a group of police officers from Scotland Yard's Drugs Squad were searching a large scrap yard in Dalston, a poor inner city district of East London. The officers were looking for pills. The yard, which was between railway viaducts, covered some three acres of ground. It was littered with stacks of steel pipes and girders, piles of scaffolding, and the wrecks of motor vehicles. Small fires were lit here and there, filling the air with an acrid stench. The officers, led by Detective Inspector Ian Malone, gingerly picked their way between the oily puddles and rusted metal towards the yard's prefab two-storey offices. The owner of the yard was a man named Jimmy Knight, who they knew to be a very wealthy man. He had made a fortune out of the scrap metal business and had put the money into a leisure complex in Stanmore, North London. The officers thought, wrongly as it later turned out, that Jimmy's scrap yard was being used to manufacture and hide drugs destined for the club scene.

They knew that Jimmy Knight had two younger brothers, John and Ronnie. Two other brothers had died some years beforehand. one murdered in a vicious Soho brawl, the other was struck down by a tumour on the brain. John was quiet and kept himself to himself, seemingly to all outward appearances a respectable businessman. Among other things he ran a garage in North London. Ronnie, by contrast, was a very public figure. He was married to an actress, Barbara Windsor, from the Carry On films, and owned a nightclub in the West End. The officers strode into Jimmy Knight's large untidy office, where they found six chairs roughly arranged to form a semicircle around his desk. It was as if a meeting had been in progress and had been quickly broken up, possibly when the officers had been seen at the yard gates. Plastic cups half-full of warm tea were on the desk. To the officers' minds, whoever had been there, had left in rather a hurry. Jimmy had nothing to say, but the officers' suspicions were heightened and they found five smartly dressed men lurking in a room nearby behind a locked door. The men, all in their forties, had an air of self-confidence about them that, to the experienced officers, spoke volumes. They'd seen it all before, something was not right, the five were highly evasive and reluctant to tell the police what they were doing at the yard. So the officers took down their details. One man turned out to be a wealthy north London property dealer called Terry

133

Perkins.(see Hatton Garden section) Another man, John Mason, ran a nearby launderette and was there with his mate, Ronnie Everett, the landlord of a pub in the Grays Inn Road. Another man tried to give the police a false name and address, but he was quickly recognised by one of the officers, as Billy Hickson. His real identity was confirmed after further questioning at a local police station. Hickson had done time for armed robbery. The fifth man was Jimmy Knight's younger brother, John. It was all very intriguing. The officers knew that the Knight family had some heavy connections, but they were surprised at the set of people they had found hiding in that room. All of the men had form in one way or another, what was going on?

During the thorough search of the yard a box was found containing some specialist glassware, the kind one might use for the chemical synthesis of drugs and Jimmy Knight was arrested and charged but later acquitted. He told the magistrates that the glassware belonged to someone else in the yard. Jimmy said he knew nothing about it. 'How should I know what goes on. All I do is rent out the lock-ups. What the men do inside them is their own business.' Despite the police's suspicions, the five men meeting at the yard that day had done nothing wrong. But still, the meeting was duly logged by the officers. The men's names were added to the Drugs Squad's intelligence database, purely for its own internal use and no more was thought of it. That was until Easter Monday 1983.

John and Ronnie Knight grew up during and after the Second World War in Dalston, a poor area of East London. John began thieving at the tender age of ten, and by his early twenties, he had his own 'firm', which specialized in stealing goods from parked-up lorries. Ronnie married Barbara Windsor, a rising star of the stage, whom he had met through Reggie Kray. He set up clubs and businesses, some legal, most not, in London's West End. Elder brother Jimmy went into the scrap metal business, as did two other brothers, Billy and David.

In 1969 Billy died of a brain tumor, and, the following year, tragedy again struck the family when David was stabbed to death in a vicious club-land brawl. Ronnie was later accused of arranging the murder of the man who had killed David. By the end of the 1970s, John, Ronnie, and Jimmy, were wealthy men. John owned a pub, a large repair garage, a beautiful house in the Herefordshire countryside and, with Ronnie, a sumptuous Spanish villa. Mingling with villains and stars alike, Ronnie was by now earning a fortune from his illicit businesses. Although John and Jimmy kept well away from the limelight, Ronnie, through his turbulent relationship with Barbara Windsor, had become something of a celebrity himself. Despite John Knight's apparent success in business, he had one burning ambition – to pull off the perfect crime.

Watching a Security Express van unload one day in his local high street, he hatched the idea of carrying out an audacious raid on the van's depot in Curtain Road, London EC1. The raid needed careful planning, so John found a secret vantage point, from which he and other members of his hand-picked team of professional armed robbers could observe the comings and goings at the depot without being seen. Through a mixture of observation and inside information, John worked out the daily routines of the guards, and, over the course of more than a year, identified the depot's security flaws.

He discovered that the depot was most vulnerable early in the morning, when the sole guard on duty would routinely leave the depot by the back door and walk across the yard to get a pint of milk left outside the gate, meaning he had to open the gate! John laid plans to carry out his raid on Easter Monday 1983 and in the small hours the gang silently moved into position, hiding behind large industrial bins. They lay in wait for the lone guard on duty to come out and open the gate to get the milk. When he did, they pounced, bundling him back inside and into the depot building.

The gang made the guard sit at his control desk as normal and explain how the controls worked. Two armed robbers crouched underneath the desk to make sure he co-operated. The guard let the rest of the staff into the depot as usual. But as they walked through the security doors, one by one, they were taken hostage at gun-point, frog-marched downstairs to the guards' locker room, and tied up.

Detective Inspector Peter Wilton had worked his way up through the ranks of the police, and, in 1980, had been placed in charge of a Flying Squad team based in East London. Because of the size of the Security Express robbery Peter Wilton's team was called in to investigate. Wilton's officers arrived on the scene to find not a single clue left behind. Some £6 million pounds in cash was missing from the vaults. Lengthy interviews with the shaken guards provided little to go on. The gang had spoken with fake Irish accents and had worn masks and helmets throughout. For months the Flying Squad's investigation floundered. That summer, acting on tip-offs from underworld sources, the Flying Squad started surveillance operations on men thought likely to have committed the robbery.

The Flying Squad's big breakthrough came the following year, in January 1984, when they arrested a man named John Horsley who had been observed meeting several suspected robbers. Horsley confessed that he had helped the robbers hide sacks of money in his garage. He also told the Flying Squad that he had built a cupboard with a false back at his father-in-law's flat, so that he could hide £270,000 in cash on behalf of one of the robbers, Billy Hickson. Horsley's statement was dynamite and he agreed to turn Queens Evidence. However, he soon retracted his statement, pleading guilty to robbery. Police believe someone had threatened his family. This left the Flying Squad almost back where they started. At the trial Horsley was described by the Judge as the gang's 'banker' and jailed for eight years.

Alan and Linda Opiola were close to John Knight. In fact they were so close that they would often come around for dinner at the Knight's grand house in the Hertfordshire countryside. Alan Opiola ran a garage in North London and John Knight trusted him implicitly. But in that, John made a fatal error of judgment. In February 1984 the Flying Squad hauled Opiola in over some suspicious van hire documents they had uncovered. After some tough questioning Opiola sought a deal if he told what he knew about John Knight. A deal was offered and he and Linda both agreed to become Supergrasses. It was the big breakthrough the Flying Squad had long been waiting for.

The Opiolas told the Flying Squad how they had helped John Knight sort out robbery cash in their master bedroom. They were immediately taken into protective custody, and, after Knight's conviction, given new identities under a witness protection program. In December 1984, Flying Squad officers broke through a false wall at Knight's East London pub The Fox and discovered a secret compartment, which they suspected had been used to store robbery cash. The secret compartment smelt of old beer and mildew and this later became significant 'evidence' at the trial of the gang. It was claimed that some of the notes that police had recovered smelt the same, and therefore must have been stored at the Fox. The pub had previously been managed by Clifford Saxe, on behalf of John Knight. In 1983 Saxe gave up the tenancy of the pub and retired to the Costa del Sol, where he remained until his death in March 2002. In December 2000 police had questioned him again over the Security Express robbery but he was by then considered too ill to be extradited.

Arrests were made and convictions were secured largely on the basis of the evidence from Alan Opiola. Ronnie Knight fled to Spain the evening of his brother's arrest and was to stay out of reach of the arms of the Law for the next eight years, protected by the extradition arrangements then in force between Britain and Spain. He was dubbed by the Press 'Britain's most wanted man'. The Flying Squad continued to gather evidence against him and other suspected robbers living on the Costa del Sol. In Spain he married his new love, Sue Haylock, and together they ran an Indian restaurant named Mumtaz and an eponymous nightclub, RKnights, the scene of violent crimes including a physical attack upon Knight, but by the mid-1990s, he was in financial difficulties and in 1993 Ronnie decided that enough was enough and made arrangements to come home. He arrived at Luton airport, to be greeted on the tarmac by the Flying Squad. He was jailed for seven years in January 1995 for handling £300,000 in stolen money from the £6m armed robbery at the Security Express depot. He said he was not involved in the robbery, and the prosecution counsel Michael Worsley QC agreed the charge should remain on file, but Knight did plead guilty to handling the stolen bank notes. Judge Gerald Gordon said when sentencing Knight 'Clearly, I do not know what precise role you played. But professional robbers such as those involved are not going to hand over the sort of sums you got unless the person to whom they give it is very deeply involved himself'.

David, John Knight's brother, was fatally stabbed by Alfredo Zomparelli, who himself was murdered in 1974 after being released following a prison sentence for manslaughter. Zomparelli had pleaded self-defence. After hit-man George Bradshaw confessed to his involvement, and alleged Knight had paid him £1,000 to kill Zomparelli, Knight was arrested for the murder of Zomparelli and tried at the Old Bailey in 1980 and was acquitted. In his later *Memoirs and*

Confessions (1998), Knight said he had hired a different hit-man, Nicky Gerard, to carry out the killing in payback for the murder of his brother. Under the double jeopardy rules in force at the time, it meant he could not be tried a second time, although Knight again denied responsibility in 2002. Gerard, later also murdered, was acquitted at the same trial as Knight.

The last I heard of John Knight he was living in Luton and Ronnie was in sheltered housing.

****

CHAPTER 19

1987 KNIGHTSBRIDGE SAFE DEPOSIT ROBBERY

The Knightsbridge Security Deposit robbery took place on 12 July 1987 in Cheval Place, Knightsbridge which is part of the City of Westminster in London. It is a very high class and expensive area with the Harrods store as its focal point. This robbery, the Banco Central robbery at Fortaleza, and the $900 million stolen from the Central Bank of Iraq in 2003 are said to be the largest bank robberies in history up to that date.

The robbery was led by Valerio Viccei (1955–2000), a lawyer's son who arrived in London in 1986 from his native Italy where he was already an established criminal and wanted for 50 armed robberies. Once in London, he quickly resumed his robbery career to fund his playboy lifestyle. He rented a smart flat in St John's Wood and soon had a string of glamorous blondes in tow, he dined at the best restaurants and drove around the city in a gleaming Ferrari. He funded his playboy lifestyle by doing what he knew best, robbing banks. He was responsible for the first successful raid on the Queen's Bank, Coutts.

For the Knightsbridge Vault robbery he secured inside help from the managing director of the centre, Parvez Latif, a cocaine user, who was heavily in Viccei's debt. On the day of the robbery, two men entered the Knightsbridge Safe Deposit Centre and requested to rent a safe deposit box. After being shown down and into the vault, they produced handguns and subdued the manager and security guards. The thieves then hung a sign on the street-level door explaining that the Centre was closed, and let in further accomplices. They got away with a haul of gold, gems and priceless goods. The haul was so vast that Viccei filled his bath with banknotes and glittering jewels covered the floor of his flat in Hampstead, North London. One diamond alone was worth over 4 million pounds. They broke open many of the safe deposit boxes and left with a hoard estimated to be worth £60 million the inflation adjusted value would be £135 million today, 2021. However, the true value of the haul was only estimated, as those renting the boxes may have, for various reasons, not accurately reported the stolen contents and more than 30 key holders failed to come forward at all. One hour after the robbers departed, the shift changed and the new staff discovered the crime alerted the police. Police forensic investigators recovered a bloody fingerprint that was traced to Valerio Viccei. Several of his accomplices were arrested during a series of coordinated raids in London and the outskirts on 12th August 1987 and they were later convicted of the crime. Viccei, however had fledto Latin America. Later, when his oversized ego got the better of his common sense he returned to England to retrieve and ship his Ferrari Testarossato Latin America and police arrested him by blocking the road and smashing the front windscreen of his car before dragging him out of it. Viccei was sentenced to 22 years, serving his sentence in Parkhurst Prison on the Isle of White. While serving his sentence there, he forged a friendship with Dick Leach, a Flying Squad officer who led his arrest. They regularly wrote letters to each other, referring to themselves as Fred (Leach) and Garfield or The Wolf (Viccei). In 1992, he was deported to Italy to serve the rest of his sentence and face charges there. He was incarcerated in an open jail in Pescara, where he was allowed to live the luxury lifestyle he was accustomed to, as well as running a translation company from the cell. Thanks to an Italian policy of semi-liberty, he was allowed to do as he pleased, as long as he returned to his cell at night. Italian Police officers kept an eye on him when he went out and became suspicious when they spotted a stolen Lancia Thema on a dirt track in the countryside near Ascoli at around 11.30 in the morning. Viccei and Mafia mobster Antonio Maletesta were standing by the car when the officers stopped and asked them for their documents. Maletesta ran off, but Viccei pulled out his semi-automatic Magnum 357 handgun. Policeman Enzo Baldini jumped on him and in the struggle both men were shot. The police officer was hit in the groin by a bullet and recovered in hospital after emergency surgery. But Viccei was killed instantly when a burst of bullets from Baldini's machine gun ripped through him. He was dragged into the car by one of his henchmen and the vehicle sped off. But when his gang realised he was dead, they dumped him and the car on a road in Teramo, 100 miles east of Rome. Ski masks and other items found in the car led the police to think that he and his Mafia friends were planning a kidnapping or bank job.

In a British TV documentary, Viccei was filmed in Italy boasting about his lifestyle and his many sexual conquests, which included Lady Bienvenida Buck wife of Tory MP Sir Anthony Buck.

She was the glamorous blonde Spanish mistress whose kiss-and-tell confession ended the career of Britain's military Defence Chief of Staff Sir Peter Harding, who commanded the RAF's combat operations in the Gulf War, which sent shockwaves around the establishment. She had a passionate affair with Viccei and they were often seen arm-in-arm in London's top nightclubs and restaurants. But the good life came to an abrupt end for Viccei when he was caught and jailed for the Knightsbridge raid.

And, even then, Lady Buck regularly visited him in maximum-security Parkhurst Prison, on the Isle of Wight. She even talked the man she later married into helping switch her former lover to a jail in his Italian homeland. Tory MP Sir Antony Buck, said 'Viccei spent the abundant time he had on his hands after being arrested writing to her. I never met him, but I contacted the Home Office to see about him being repatriated.' Viccei repaid her loyalty by staying silent over their relationship, even in his memoirs. In his book, Viccei thanked the lawyers and judges who had helped his repatriation to Italy. He added 'The same is true of Sir Antony and Lady Bienvenida Buck. She, in particular, is a good friend whose loyalty has not wavered, regardless of possible embarrassment and criticism.' Viccei, who would have been due for parole in 2003, was proud of his criminal expertise. He said 'The best job I did without question was Knightsbridge, it was magic, wonderful, when I saw all that money and jewellery I really thought I'd done it.' When asked about the missing millions, he simply smirked and shrugged his shoulders but he is believed to have secreted a huge stash of the stolen money and valuables in bank accounts and safety deposit boxes throughout the world. He even wrote to the police chief who trapped him wishing he could be at the auction of unclaimed loot from the vault's floor where it had landed as the boxes were rifled. He wrote to Detective Inspector Richard Leach from his Italian jail 'If I had my way I would be there bidding.' And he added that he would have bid for a gold shotgun pendant 'as a memento'

*************************.

CHAPTER 20

1990: £292m CITY BONDS ROBBERY

At 9.30am on May 2 1990, John Goddard, a 58-year-old messenger with the money broker Sheppards, was mugged at knifepoint on a quiet side street in the City of London. Goddard was carrying Bank of England Treasury bills and certificates of deposit from banks and building societies. The bonds were in bearer form and as good as cash to anyone holding them. The mugger escaped with 301 Treasury bills and certificates of deposit, mostly for £1m each, and the total haul was £292m.

Keith Cheeseman later received a six and a half-year jail sentence for his part in the robbery. Four other people in Britain were charged with handling the bonds, but were acquitted after the highly unusual step of offering no evidence was taken at the opening of their 1991 trials. Police believed the City mugging was carried out by Patrick Thomas, a petty crook from south London. This is also what petty thief Johnny Tippett says in his autobiography saying that he met Thomas shortly after the robbery and Thomas showed him the bonds. His story is that Thomas had been paid by a bigger international crime gang and did the job on their behest as being a lower echelon criminal it would appear to the police as a chance mugging if he was caught. Thomas, who was found dead from a gunshot wound to the head in December 1991, was never charged with the robbery. His death has been linked to his liking for cocaine and the his inability to keep his mouth shut about the bonds when high. The rumour mill was rife about the crime and suggests it was a City futures dealer who passed insider information out to an Irish gang that was involved and with Thomas getting more and more 'big headed' about his part and talking about it and spending an awful lot of money the police were getting very interested in him and it was decided to 'shut him up for good'. He was found in his south London home with a gunshot wound to the head. The bonds started turning up in the USA being hawked around by known fraudster Keith Cheeseman which brought the attention of the FBI to the case in conjunction with the Met.

Cheeseman had a varied con man career once buying football club Dunstable Town FC with the proceeds of a previous fraud. The club was forced into liquidation in 1977. City of London police and the FBI had infiltrated the gang involved in laundering the bonds in the USA and Cheeseman was trapped in the USA by the FBI with fellow fraudster Mark Lee Osborne a Texan businessman who had tried to sell some of the bonds to undercover officers posing as Mafia buyers. Cheeseman fled to Tenerife where he was arrested and sent back to the USA. He said he had fled in fear for his life as he had been told there was a Mafia contract out on him. He could be right as Mark Lee Osborne's body was found in the boot of a car in Houston, Texas with two bullets in his head. The police recovered all but two of the 301 bonds thanks to an informant which it is alleged could have been Osborne after a 'deal' was made. Cheeseman had a failed attempt in the past to defraud a city company of £8m by seducing Elaine Borg, a computer supervisor at the company and persuading her to transfer £8m of client's money to an offshore account. City of London Fraud Squad were watching and although Cheeseman avoided arrest Borg didn't and got 18months suspended.

****

CHAPTER 21

1995 MIDLAND BANK CENTRE SALFORD

An ex-policeman who became the 'inside man' for a robbery gang was convicted of plotting one of Europe's biggest ever cash raids at the Midland Bank Clearing Centre in Salford. Armoured vehicle driver Graham Huckerby, 41, took a £2,500 bribe to let masked gunmen hijack his bullet and bomb-proof Securicor vehicle, kidnap him and steal £6.6m.

He was among 12 people arrested in August 1999 after a four year police investigation and numerous court hearings which cost an estimated £10m. During the raid itself, the gunmen left Huckerby gagged with tape and handcuffed to railings before snatching £4m in cash and £2m in cheques. Huckerby later spun a web of deceit telling police he had been 'terrified' at being kidnapped and held against his will. But after the raid in July 1995, at the Midland Bank Clearing Centre in Salford, Huckerby, who had several debts, mortgage and child maintenance arrears, suddenly enjoyed a change of fortunes and them all off. He began to enjoy a jet-set lifestyle, took a three-week trip to America and made a series of large bank deposits. Police, who suspected Huckerby's account was false, were tipped off that the raid was organised by London's East End gangs who in turn recruited Greater Manchester hoodlums, probably the Noonans, to join in. Despite the arrests, the haul has never been recovered. Police fear the loot may have been too hot to launder in bank accounts in large amounts and could have been buried at secret locations for collection in years to come.

At Minshull Street Crown Court, Manchester, Huckerby, of Clifton Road, Prestwich, fell to his knees and shouted 'What have you done to me?' at the jury as he was convicted by a unanimous verdict of conspiracy to rob after a two month retrial. James Power, 58, of Hornby Street, Bury, an accomplice described as Huckerby's 'handler' was also convicted of conspiracy and got 14 years. On appeal Huckerby's sentence was squashed on account of his 'post traumatic stress. 'The court heard the robbers used a white Ford Transit as a 'cash transporter' after it was stolen earlier in London and given false registration plates.

As Huckerby and his colleague arrived at the Salford banking centre in the Security Van on the Monday to deposit weekend takings from Manchester stores, two masked men used ladders to scale a wall next to a railway line and dropped into the centre's yard. They sprinted to the van after Huckerby's colleague had gone inside the building to check in the delivery and got into his van. Huckerby failed to raise any alarm and instead drove off to a cul-de- sac followed by the gang's stolen white transit van. There he was bound and gagged. In all, 29 pillow case-sized cash bags were transferred to the Transit, which was driven to another rendezvous before the gang transferred the cash to another vehicle and scattering in a fleet of cars. They left £1m behind in the Securicor van. The whole raid was caught on video and a reward of £250,000 was offered by Securicor and Greater Manchester Police for the capture of the gang. Investigations later revealed Huckerby had accepted the £2,500 bribe to be in on the July 1995 raid. Police then engaged an undercover policeman known only as Barry to go to pubs and bookmakers in the area where Huckerby lived and play the part of a Securicor driver with a grudge against the company. The operation was designed to see if one of Huckerby's pals would plan a similar robbery with a Securicor driver as an 'inside man' again and James Power, took the bait in taped conversations boasting about the previous one and how easy it was to do. No other accomplices were ever arrested.

****

CHAPTER 22

THE BIRMINGHAM FEWTRELLS

This section on the Fewtrells is a bit 'out of course' with the rest of the book as the Fewtrell brothers were 'brummy' business men and not criminals. But it is interesting as it sheds a light on the type of business that appealed to certain 'geezers' in the 1960s, especially Nightclubs where they would have a ready market for their amphetamine and cocaine sales teams to operate in. Gangs like the Krays used their muscle and violent reputation to take over many clubs. But when the Krays tried to take over the Birmingham club scene which would have given them a stranglehold on the Midlands and a halfway warehouse on the route to the 2nd biggest drugs market in the UK, Manchester, they bit off more than they could chew.

Mention the surname Fewtrell to anyone in Birmingham and chances are they will know exactly who you are talking about, because for four decades the colorful family, including brothers Eddie, Don and Chris, entertained the city and became the Kings of Clubland. Eddie, affectionately known as 'Mr Nightclub', sold his empire more than 25 years ago, but the Fewtrell name has never lost its place in the minds of the Birmingham public. The Fewtells kept the Krays out of Birmingham.

Their story is a real-life rags-to-riches tale which started in the back streets of Aston. Eddie, one of eight brothers, broke onto the nightclub scene in the 50s with his brother Chris when they bought the old Victoria Cafe, in Navigation Street, and turned it into the Bermuda Club. In an instant the venue transformed nightlife in the city which, until then, had just been a collection of coffee shops and espresso bars. In 1960, Eddie and Don went into business opening the Cedar Club on Constitution Hill.

Among the live acts who performed was up-and-coming star Tom Jones, who performed for two nights – for just £70. But as the brother's empire grew, they attracted the attention of two of Britain's most notorious gangsters – the Krays. In an interview seven years ago, Eddie recounted the time the East Enders tried to muscle in on the Birmingham club scene – and were sent packing. He recalled: "I was in the club one night when some bloke came up to me and said that he knew some people who might be able to help me out. Well I was getting a bit annoyed at this point, here's some cockney telling me he knows people who can look after me and I'm thinking what do I need their help for when I've got seven brothers to do that? I grew up fighting around the streets of Aston and in the army and so on and I wasn't having any of that so I told him in no uncertain terms to clear off.'

(RUMOUR HAS IT THAT A FIGHT BETWEEN THE TWO TOOK PLACE IN EDDIE'S OFFICE AND RELIABLE(?) WITNESSES HAVE TOLD HOW A GUN WAS PRODUCED BY THE COCKNEY AND THE STRUGGLE ENDED WITH HIS EAR BEING HALF SHOT OFF.)

'There were threats and so on after that and some trouble, so I went to the chief of police in Birmingham and told him what was happening. He told me to sort it out so we did, and that was the end of that.'

(THE 'SORTING OUT' BECAME KNOWN AS THE BATTLE OF SNOW HILL. SEE FURTHER DOWN PAGE.)

The brothers' business careers went their separate ways in the 1970s. Eddie opened Boogies nightclub, Boogies Brasserie, Edwards No 7, Edwards No 8, the Paramount pub, Goldwyns nightclub and Abigails, while Don owned The Revolution, later known as Pollyannas in Newhall Street, and also Faces at Five Ways. He sold his clubs in the mid 80s and went to Australia but returned two years later when he rejoined Eddie's empire, managing Goldwyns. The link-up ended when Eddie sold up to Ansells Brewery in a multi-million deal in the early 90s. Eddie though, found he could not stay away from the club scene and, as soon as a golden handcuffs clause in the deal expired, he bought clubs in Birmingham and Merry Hill. In 1993, Don, then 63, revealed he was broke and living in a council flat. He reflected in an interview: 'All sorts of things have been said about the Fewtrells. But we have given a lot of people a lot of pleasure and we changed the face of Birmingham. I've had the money and it's gone. But I'm a happy man and you can't take it with you when you go.'

Chris died in 1999, aged 56, after a long battle with cancer. Of the other brothers, Frank died of a heart attack, aged just 35, and Ken also died, aged 56.

The Battle of Snow Hill

They gathered in large numbers under the shadow of the sodium lights that fringed Snow Hill Station. Hundreds of bear-like, brooding individuals with noses bent and broken more times than politicians' promises. On one side, the Kray Twins' army of Cockney villains. On the other, the Fewtrells doormen. It was a blood-spattered brawl involving the hardest men spat out of London's East End and the Second City's tough Aston District bouncers that, for those involved, will forever be remembered as The Battle of Snow Hill. And for Ronnie and Reggie, the savage, final chapter in their feud with the vast Fewtrell clan had special significance. The late 1960s explosion of violence took place on October 14th, the date of the Battle of Hastings. Ronnie delighted in pointing that out when recalling the carnage. And like Harold's Saxon hordes, the notorious Cockney villains were crushed, their bid to spread the criminal cancer of drugs, extortion and crime to Birmingham streets forever thwarted.

IT IS RUMOURED THAT SEVERAL BODIES FROM THE BATTLE OF SNOW HILL ARE ENTOMBED IN THE GIANT CEMENT PILLARS HOLDING UP SPAGHETTI JUNCTION BUT I DON'T THINK THE CONSTRUCTION DATES AND THE BATTLE DATES CORRESPOND. A book has been written by David Keogh, married to Eddie Fewtrell's daughter, Abi and it includes recollections from the brothers. It recounts the dark days when the Krays attempted to make Birmingham their manor. David admits he's used some poetic licence, changing names and locations and adding drama to produce a Pulp Fiction style. But the incidents, are firmly embedded in fact, he insisted, gained through interviews and the family conversations. David, who lives in Plymouth, reveals how the Krays gave the order for Eddie – regarded as the figurehead of the family, to be killed. They hired a hitman to rub-out the nightspot boss in his own club. In the life-and-death struggle, the gunman – a cockney – had his ear shot off as we have already mentioned from another source so it seems to be correct.

The simmering ill-will between the two families was spawned by a simple misunderstanding. The Fewtrells wrongly believed Ronnie and Reggie had organised the trashing of one of their businesses. 'They just wanted to run clubs and make money. They wanted to be successful businessmen. The incident with the gun gave that feel to the family and they couldn't shake it off. The guy tried to shoot him and Eddie tried to wrestle the gun off him,' explained David. 'In the struggle, it kept firing and the guy had his ear shot off. Everyone thought Eddie had shot one of the Krays. That's where the reputation came from.'

There is one undeniable truth. The Fewtrells – Eddie, Roger, Chrissy, Frankie, Johnny, Don and Gordon were tough individuals who refused to be bullied, not even by the curdled cream of London's organised crime scene. One other brother, Kenny, did not follow the clubland tradition and became something of a loner. Chrissy, in particular, was a talented boxer tipped for big things in the pro ranks. In Aston, everyone knew the Fewtrells. Dad George was a larger than life individual who held the dubious distinction of being the last man in Birmingham arrested for being drunk in charge of a horse.

Eddie worked in the rag market before purchasing his first venue, The Bermuda Club. 'His wife Hazel persuaded Eddie to get the club, she was the very much behind a lot of what the Fewtrells did. She was the driving force.' The Bermuda Club, in the winter of 1961, was to be the setting for the Fewtrells first fateful meeting with Ronnie and Reggie.

It was explosive and lit the touchpaper to a turbulent turf war that would last years.

'At the time the Elbow Room, in Aston, was popular with Londoners, particularly London gangsters,' says David. 'There's a photograph of the Kray Twins in Aston. I believe they were on their way to the Elbow Room when they turned-up at the Bermuda Club.' The twins brought their brash reputation into the Bermuda. Swaggering, demanding and intimidating, they were red-rag to Brummie bull, Eddie.

'The conversation was getting heavy. The insults began to fly,' said David. 'It was getting close to a fight.' The incendiary encounter ended with something that would've never happened to Ronnie and Reggie in the heart of London. They were thrown out. Soon after the villains' enforced exit, the club was hit, and hit hard, by a notorious gang known as The Meat Market Mob, a title bestowed on the gang through their weapons of choice, meat cleavers. 'The Krays had nothing to do with it, I believe, says David. 'The Meat Market Mob and the Fewtrells had bad blood between them. It was a vicious fight and a lot of people were injured.'

In a bid to bring the Fewtrells to heel and teach them a painful lesson the Krays dispatched lieutenants Chris and Tony Lambrianou (see section on them) to carry out their dirty work. They were waiting outside the Cedar Club in Ronnie Kray's Jag and spotted Don. They bit off a lot more than they could chew, heading back home bloody and bruised. The stage was set for the Snow Hill showdown, a battle that many have dismissed as a myth.

'Did it happen?' smiles David. 'I've spoken to 50 guys who say they were there and 50 who said it didn't happen. I've spoken to doormen who are adamant they were there. The brothers I've spoken to refuse to say anything. In Birmingham, the tip-off came from the Irish community. They liked the Fewtrells because, at the time, there were clubs you could not get into with an Irish accent. They were welcomed by the Fewtrells. They were told the Krays were gathering by friends and colleagues in London on the grapevine and passed it on.' It is, David insisted, thanks to the brothers that Birmingham did not endure the Krays' brutal reign, although it's a part of Birmingham's past the prime-players do not dwell on. In a 2001 interview, Eddie, living in quiet retirement and breeding horses near Ledbury, touched on the subject. He said: 'I was in the club one night when some bloke came up to me and said that he knew some people who might be able to help me out the rest is history.' In 1993, the late Don Fewtrell reflected on the family's lasting legacy. "All sorts of things have been said about the Fewtrells. But we have given a lot of people a lot of pleasure and we changed the face of Birmingham."

And they saved it from the Krays.

****

CHAPTER 23

2009 GRAFF DIAMOND JEWELLERS

The Graff Diamonds robbery took place on 6 August 2009 when two men posing as customers entered the premises of Graff Diamonds in New Bond Street, London and stole jewellery worth nearly £40 million (US$65 million). It was believed to be the largest ever gems heist in Britain at the time and the second largest British robbery after the £53 million raid on the Kent Securitas depot in 2006. The thieves' haul totalled 43 items of jewellery, consisting of rings, bracelets, necklaces and wristwatches. One necklace alone has been reported as being worth more than £3.5m Britain's previous largest jewellery robbery also took place at Graff's, in 2003. As of today none of the stolen jewels have been recovered.

The robbers used the services of a professional make-up artist to alter their skin tones and their features using latex prosthetics and were fitted with professional wigs. The artist took four hours to apply the disguises having been told that it was for a music video. Viewing the results in a mirror, robber Aman Kassaye commented 'My own mother wouldn't recognise me now,' to which his accomplice is reported to have laughed and replied 'That's got to be a good thing, hasn't it?' The same make-up studio had unwittingly helped members of the gang that robbed the Securitas Depot in 2006.On the day of the robbery at 4.40 pm, two sharply dressed men arrived at the Graff Diamonds jewellery store by

taxi and once inside produced two handguns which they used to threaten staff. They made no attempt to conceal their faces from the premises' CCTV cameras due to their elaborate disguises. Petra Ehnar, a shop assistant, was forced at gunpoint to empty the store's display cabinets. A total of 43 rings, bracelets, necklaces and watches were taken. She was briefly held hostage at gunpoint and was forced into the street during the getaway. She testified that the robbers told her that she would be killed if she did not carry out their demands. After releasing her outside the store, one of the robbers fired a shot into the air to create public confusion, and both escaped the scene in a blue BMW car. This vehicle was abandoned in nearby Dover Street, where a second gunshot was fired into the ground while the robbers switched to a silver Mercedes. They again switched vehicles in Farm Street, after which there was no further information regarding their whereabouts.

All of the diamonds had been laser-inscribed with the Graff logo and a Germological Institute of America identification number. Detectives investigating the robbery said 'They knew exactly what they were looking for and we suspect they already had a market for the jewels.' The suspects' details were circulated to Border Control but police believed they would have an elaborately prepared escape route and had already left the country. The robbery was being investigated by Barnes Flying Squad, headed by Detective Chief Inspector Pam Mace. Since none of the stolen jewellery was recovered Graff Diamonds, owned by the billionaire Laurence Graff, lost more than US$10 million (£6.6 million) as a result of the robbery. The actual value of the pieces for insurance purposes, was put at $39 million (£26 million). But according to Nicholas Paine, the company secretary, the syndicate that insured Graff was only liable for $28.9 million.

The robbers were caught shortly after police searched one of the getaway cars they abandoned. A pay-as-you go mobile phone was discovered that robbers Aman Kassaye and Craig Calderwood inadvertently left there after ramming into a black cab. After the collision, in their haste to transfer to a second vehicle, the robbers forgot the mobile phone. Anonymous numbers stored on it quickly allowed police to discover their identities. On 20 August 2009, two men, Craig Calderwood, 26, of no fixed address, and Solomun Beyene, 24, of Lilestone Road, London NW8, were charged in connection with the robbery. On 21 August, a third man, Clinton Mogg, 42, of Westby Road, Bournemouth, was also charged, and Calderwood and Beyene were remanded in custody by Westminster Magistrates' Court. On 22 August, Mogg appeared at Westminster Magistrates' Court. All three were remanded in custody to appear at Kingston Crown Court on 1st September. A fourth man, aged 50, was arrested and bailed. By mid-October, ten male suspects had been arrested in connection with the robbery. Charges brought against the individuals include conspiracy with others to commit robbery, attempted murder, holding someone hostage, possessing firearms and using a handgun to resist arrest. Aman Kassaye, who planned and executed the heist, was found guilty of conspiracy to rob, kidnap and possession of a firearm after a three-month trial at Woolwich Crown Court. On 7th August 2010, he was sentenced to 23 years in prison. Three other men, Solomun Beyene, 25, of London, Clinton Mogg, 43, of Bournemouth, and Thomas Thomas,

46, of Kingston upon Thames were each jailed for 16 years after also being convicted of conspiracy to rob. Craig Calderwood was finally jailed for 21 years. Experts believe the jewellery was probably been broken up so the precious stones could be anonymously resold after being recut and the Graff logos removed.

PREVIOUS ROBBERIES AT GRAFF

Graff Diamonds has been the target of several previous high-profile robberies.

In 1980, two Chicago-based gangsters armed with a handgun and a hand grenade stole jewellery valued at £1.5 million from the Sloane Street premises. Mafiosi Joseph Scalise and Arthur Rachel, who took 'less than a minute' to commit the crime, were apprehended eleven hours later in the United States and extradited to England where they were tried, convicted and imprisoned for nine years. Their haul had included the 26 carat Marlborough Diamond, worth £400,000 at the time, which has never been recovered.

In 1993, the firm's Hatton Garden workshop premises was robbed of jewellery valued at £7 million. The robbery was attributed to a group of armed robbers known as The Rascal Gang due to the Bedford Rascal vans they used.

In 2003, the New Bond Street premises was robbed by two men from the Serbian Pink Panthers international jewel thief network who stole 47 pieces of jewellery worth £23 million.

In 2005, three armed robbers stole jewellery valued at £2 million from the Sloane Street premises.

In 2007, two robbers, who arrived at the Sloane Street premises in a chauffeur-driven Bentley Continental Flying Spur threatened staff at gunpoint and stole jewellery worth £10 million. In the same year, the Graff premises in Wafi City, Dubai was targeted by the Pink Panthers again, using two Audi A8 cars to carry out a ramraid, Jewellery worth AED14.7 million (£2.4 million) was taken, although later recovered when two of the gang, both Serbians, were arrested.

****

CHAPTER 24
ALBERT DIMES

Born in Hamilton, South Lanarkshire to an Italian father and Scottish mother, Albert Dimes moved to London with his family and grew up in Clerkenwell which was dubbed 'Little Italy' at the time. He went on to work for gang leader William 'Billy' Hill, who was involved in bookmaking and loan sharking during the 1940s and 1950s. (see earlier section)

In July 1941 Dimes was convicted with Joseph Collette of attacking Edward Fletcher at a Soho Club in Wardour Street. The Recorder noted that the incident took place 'under the shadow of a graver offence. One man had lost his life and another man was under sentence of death.' He dismissed any prejudice against second generation Italians. Harry Capocci was acquitted and Dimes was bound over for three years. In the same incident, Harry 'Little Harry' Distleman was stabbed to death by Antonio Mancini. In August 1955, Dimes was arrested with rival gangster Jack Spot during a knife fight in Soho. Neither man was charged. As a result of his arrest, Spot's power in the city's underworld declined. The battle almost spread to politics when Dimes tried to use National Labour Party members against rivals Bud Flanagan and Jack Spot, Jewish gangsters involved in funding the 43 Group.

In 1966, Dimes helped to arrange a conference between New York Mafiosi and the Corsican Francisci brothers, apparently regarding investment in London casinos. Dimes was a close associate of Charlie Richardson, who's firm's presence in Soho delayed the Kray twins from moving into the area for several years.

Dimes died in November 1972 at his home on Oakwood Avenue, Beckenham, South London from cancer. Death records exist in both his birth name of Dimeo, and the adopted Dimes. His funeral was held on 20 November 1972 in Beckenham. The Kray Twins sent a wreath that was reportedly destroyed by friends of the family who believed the association with the Krays brought shame on the family. Dimes was survived by his wife Hilda Kathleen (née Brewer), whom he married in 1939 and their 3 children Albert, Doreen and Eileen.

****

CHAPTER 25

JOHN 'GOLDFINGER' PALMER

John 'Goldfinger' Palmer had not planned to return to the UK in a Brazilian Airlines plane, economy class, but after running out of safe havens to stay in away from British Justice he had no choice. Having been slung out of Spain after being described as 'undesirable' by the Spanish Police and being refused entry to most of the 'usual' criminal bolt-holes like Panama, Colombia and most of the other South American countries that welcomed rich fugitives with plenty of bribery cash available, he had travelled from Spain to Brazil expecting to be allowed in but the British Police had been aware of his plans and had a quiet word with the Brazilian immigration department and he was refused entry. They asked him where he would like to be sent onto and as he had run out of places that might accept a man on the run who was in the top twenty most wanted list sent round by Scotland Yard, 'Goldfinger' had no alternative but to come home and face the music. Other passengers were not aware who this single traveller was until the plane taxied to a far part of Heathrow and an announcement on the speakers asked 'would passenger John Palmer please identify himself'. He raised his hand in defeat and was ushered off the aircraft by two airport security men and handed over to Scotland Yard's DS Ken John. 'You are John Palmer?' asked the Detective. 'Yes I am', replied a resigned John Palmer. The Detective then went through Palmer's addresses and previous addresses just to be sure and then arrested him for 'conspiracy with others to handle gold stolen in the Brinks-Mat bullion robbery of 1985.' Ironic that Palmer was arrested at the very airport that the gold had been stolen from. Thus began the long court room drama that ended with Palmer's acquittal and then his murder. The big boys behind the Brinks-Mat heist who are not dead are still free, some after serving a prison term but many of those who were entrusted with keeping the gold and looking after the families whilst the robbers were inside are now dead, (see the Brinks Mat section). All died in suspicious circumstances or as victims of very obvious 'hits'. With £25million involved you don't rip off anybody unless you have a death wish. Some tried, they are dead, including John Palmer. He started young, one of seven children, selling paraffin off the back of a lorry, having left school at 15 a serial truant who had not learned to read or write. He then progressed and moved on to work as a jewellery dealer in Bristol, a job that some might speculate gave him a taste for precious metals which led to his own scrap metal business, focusing on scrap gold and it is alleged much of it the stolen gold from UK robberies. He had a notice on his desk which read 'Remember the golden rule, he who has the gold makes the rules.' He was also fond of breaking them himself, going on to become one of Britain's most prolific criminals. He ran a gold and jewellery dealing company, Scadlynn Ltd, in Bedminster Bristol with business partners Garth Victor Chappell and Terence Edward James Patch.

Palmer and Chappell had been arrested in 1980 when they worked together selling furniture. The two men were charged with obtaining credit on furniture by providing false references, with Palmer receiving a six-month suspended prison sentence. But it was for his involvement in the 1983 Brink's-Mat robbery at Heathrow Airport that he became infamous and which earned him his nickname 'Goldfinger'. More than £25m worth of gold was stolen in what was considered at the time as the biggest robbery to have taken place in the UK. Mr Palmer, was said to have melted the gold down in his back garden smelter. However, he denied knowing it was stolen and was acquitted in 1987, blowing kisses to the jury from the dock when the verdict was delivered. Chappell and Patch of Scadlynn Ltd were arrested for their involvement in melting down £26 million worth of gold from the robbery to try to pass it off as legitimate. Two days after armed robbers Brian Robinson and Micky McAvoy were jailed, Chappell withdrew £348,000 from the company's accounts. Throughout their trial, a total of £1.1 million had been withdrawn. It was revealed that the company had been processing millions of pounds' worth of gold, but claimed it was gold they had purchased themselves. The company's books stated that they were selling the melted gold for virtually the same amount as they had purchased it for which didn't make sense, unless the records were false.

Confiscated documents also showed that the company had been evading tax, and were ordered for pay £80,000 in unpaid tax. Palmer evaded arrest at the time, after fleeing to Tenerife with his family just days prior to his company being raided and its directors arrested. His family returned to England an sold his remaining assets back home and he used the money to set up a timeshare business at Island Village, near Playa de las Americas.

After his return on the Brazilian Aircraft Palmer admitting to melting down gold bars from the robbery in his garden, he was acquitted during the trial in 1987 after claiming that he wasn't aware they were stolen. Chappell was sentenced to ten years in the earlier trial. Worth around £500m in today's prices, most of the gold has never been recovered and the case remains open. In the decade that followed, he seemingly managed to stay out of trouble, but it was not the case behind the scenes. He was secretly building his massive timeshare scam in Tenerife which propelled him to 105th on the Sunday Times Rich List, a position he shared with the Queen. His criminal activities netted him an estimated fortune of £300m, which he used to buy a mansion, a French chateau with its own golf course, a jet, two helicopters, a classic car collection and a yacht called the Brave Goose of Essex.

But Mr Palmer knew he was playing a risky game having left about 20,000 time share victims out of pocket, and he took to wearing body armour underneath his designer suits. He was also in direct competition with the Italian mafia on the Canaries who also ran Time Share scams in the islands and were getting very agitated with the bad publicity his empire was bringing down on the scams and the gullible public holidaymakers were getting wise. So justice eventually caught up with him and he was extradited back to the UK and he was jailed for eight years in 2001 for the Spanish scam.

Mr Palmer represented himself, his defence being he was so rich he did not need to be involved with the fraud. In 2001, he defended himself again after sacking his legal team in one of the longest fraud trials in British legal history. He was found guilty 'of masterminding the largest timeshare fraud on record' and jailed for eight years. It is reported that he swindled 20,000 people out of £30 million, but attempts by the Crown to confiscate this profit were later stopped in a court hearing. Sentenced to 8 years, he served just over half of this term. His fortune at the time of his conviction was estimated at about £300 million, but Palmer was declared bankrupt in 2005 with debts of £3.9m.

In 2007, he was arrested again on charges including fraud. Reportedly, he had been able to continue his criminal activities during his previous incarceration following his 2001 conviction. In 2009, after two years without charge in a high security Spanish jail, he was released on bail, but was required to report to court authorities every two weeks. In 2015, it was alleged by The Times from leaked Operation Tiberius files, that Palmer was protected from arrest and investigation by a clique of high-ranking corrupt Metropolitan Police officers. Palmer's companions were reportedly once detained in possession of a silenced Uzi submachine gun and 380 rounds of ammunition. Roy Ramm, ex-commander of specialist operations at the Metropolitan Police, testified against him during the trial and describes him as 'a strange man', who was well aware of the number of enemies he had accrued over the years. 'He was quite an arrogant man, which led him to dismissing his barrister,' he said.

John Palmer was murdered on 24 June 2015 at the age of 64 in his gated home at South Weald, near Brentwood by gunshot wounds to the chest. Palmer had been shot six times probably by a professional assassin using an 8mm .32 calibre pistol fitted with a silencer. The fact he had been shot 6 times was only revealed during a post-mortem as he had recently had open heart surgery which the wounds were mistaken for. It was later revealed that at the time of his death, Palmer faced charges in Spain for fraud, firearm possession and money laundering. It was only after his death that it was revealed that in addition to his activities in Spain, Palmer also opened the first Russian timeshare company in the 1990s. It was suggested that he had Soviet secret service connections, but lost the Russian business to Mafia rivals.

According to a special documentary broadcast by the BBC presented by broadcaster Roger Cook reveals that since 1999 police had run an intelligence operation on Palmer from the RAF Spadeadam base in Cumbria. Palmer was under electronic surveillance by a secret police intelligence unit for 16 years until his assassination by the hit man, according to the special BBC the Serious and Organised Crime Agency (SOCA), now the National Crime Agency had gathered intelligence on Palmer in an operation codenamed Alpine because of concerns of corruption in the Metropolitan police.

Following his death, it was revealed Palmer's partner Christina Ketley remained under police surveillance following reports from Spanish law enforcement agencies that she played a predominant role' in his criminal empire. Ketley and his mistress Saskia Mundinger, who both had children with Palmer, demanded payouts from him in 2005 to 'keep them in the lifestyle they became accustomed to'. He also had two daughters with his wife Marnie.

On 4th February 2017, a 50-year-old man was questioned on suspicion of Palmer's murder. Police said they had questioned the man who was originally from Tyneside although currently living in southern Spain. The man was not arrested but volunteered to be interviewed at a police station in the UK. The force did not specify at which police station he was interviewed. Palmer's family insists he had turned his life around by the time of his death, but he was about to stand trial and some were said to be concerned about what he would say in court and decided to silence him. Another theory is he was a police informant, which would have worried many in the underworld. Officers say his colorful past finally caught up with him in the form of a professional hit man.

Detective Chief Inspector Stephen Jennings, who was leading the investigation into the murder, said a number of lines of inquiry were focusing on Mr Palmer's 'lifestyle of criminality'. But he added 'We are not even close in terms of finishing this inquiry.' Jennings also said: 'Because of Mr Palmer's lifestyle and previous involvement in criminality, this has been a wide ranging and extensive investigation. A lot of it is based on his lifestyle. The Brinks Mat robbery 1983 was part of this.' (see that section) He was arrested and suspicion of smelting Brinks Mat gold, but never convicted of that. Jennings went on to say, 'In 2001 he was convicted of a timeshare fraud which had 16,000 potential and losses in excess of £33 million. He was sentenced to eight years in prison, so that is 16,000 potential motives.' Jennings said that at the time of his death Palmer was also being investigated by the Spanish authorities in connection with another alleged property fraud scheme and was due to stand trial in Madrid. He said police were also investigating possible links with the Hatton Garden Heist (see the section on this), Britain's biggest ever burglary, of which at least £10 million in cash, jewellery and other valuables, remain outstanding. He told the inquest 'We know he was associated with some of the individuals convicted of that crime.'

A reward to help catch the killer has been doubled to £100,000 by his family.

The story of John Palmer goes on.

****

CHAPTER 26

2015 HATTON GARDEN SAFE DEPOSIT HEIST.

This heist is the daddy of them all, bringing together many of the 'names and faces' from earlier heists in the book and showing how the London crime scene was made up of many career criminals who worked like a recruitment agency pulling together those that suited the requirements of each job dependent of their skills. I've listed the police files that show the heist from the police point of view and the actual robbery as gleaned from various reports and interviews and the aftermath. So some facts will be listed twice to maintain the time lines of the parts.

First - The police files.

On the 7th April 2015 at 8am the police were called to the Hatton Garden Safe Deposit premises after a robbery had been discovered. Straight away it was obvious that a professional team had planned and executed the heist and the flying squad were called in.

How had they managed to get a key to the front door of the premises? Could it be an inside job? That question has never been answered. Once inside the gang had forced open lift doors and climbed down the shaft to the Deposit floor which was below ground level and forced open the lift door shutter into the premises. They deactivated a very sophisticated alarm system, drilled through into the vault and opened 70 of the 999 boxes inside.

A second alarm had been triggered through to the Alarm Company HQ who sent a guard out to investigate. He checked the building found the door shut and no sign of forced entry. The company had asked for police to attend as well but they did not so the guard left and the robbers carried on.

After the robbery forensic officers drew a blank as the gang had sprayed the floors and walls with bleach which kills DNA. They had also removed the hard drives from computers linked to the internal CCTV cameras.

Let's follow the police procedure from now on...

Twenty CID officers were involved and their first breakthrough came from studying the tons of CCTV footage from numerous private systems in shops and businesses around the area.

On 2nd April at 8.20pm a white van pulled up at the kerb some yards away from the Depository. Four men got out, the driver stayed put and drove off. One man obviously aware of the CCTV surveillance carries a large bag on his shoulder blocking any view of his face. He has a key to the Depository back door and they all enter. The van's number plate is traced but is false. On the morning of Good Friday at 8am the men return to the van from inside the building, it has been pulled up to the back doorway and they drive off. They have no loot with them? This surprises the police reviewing the CCTV footage afterwards, why no loot?

On Saturday three return with a package and stay inside overnight until Sunday when they leave with several holdalls and wheelie bins full of loot which they load into the van.

Other CCTV shows a white Mercedes with two people sat in it watching the building for several days prior to the break in. This car is known to belong to a criminal called Kenny Collins. Using this car which was already known to the police was a mistake by the gang. NPR is fed into the system and the car is traced to a residence in N1 known to be Kenny Collin's house. He is now kept under surveillance. He is known as a lookout and driver in previous robberies.

Collins is identified in the CCTV of the first night of the raid as driving the van, he is with Brian Reader a well known master criminal who was heavily involved in the Brinks Mat heist and acquitted of the murder of PC John Forham. There is no sign of Reader on the second night, the Saturday, why? The reason becomes clear later when the fact that the drill being used to get through the wall from the lift corridor to the vault did its job cutting through the concrete as far as the back of the vault wall but could not get through the solid thick steel chest housing the security boxes. Reader's research had shown them to be free standing units positioned against the concrete wall which could be pushed over by using a basic builder's hydraulic joist holder on its side. It broke because the free standing units weren't free standing they were bolted into the concrete and needed more force to shift them. The job was supposed to finish that night but now to continue they needed a bigger force hydraulic wrench. The team decided to abort the mission. They argue amongst themselves. Collins, Perkins and Jones want to come back with a bigger wrench but Reader, who brought the heist together, will not defer from his one night plan. He thinks it would be too dodgy to return.

The gang splits up but Collins, Perkins, Wood and Jones

decide to go back on the Saturday with a bigger wrench and bring the fifth man into the plan with them. This is the man known as 'Basil' who the police had trouble identifying, the man with a large bag hiding his face from the outside CCTV, the man with the key and the man seen on internal CCTV disengaging the alarms. An outside light in the back entrance spooks Wood who thinks it will be noticed and he leaves.

The new wrench works and the gang push over one set of safe deposit boxes and get into the vault and open 70 boxes. They take the loot to Collins house and decide to hide it in a wheelie bin outside as Collins wife is due home and has no idea what is going on. They split it into money, gold and gems on the lounge floor. When they later go to 'divi' (divide) it Collins has passed the gems onto his brother in law Bill Lincoln to hide as he hadn't enough room in his own house, Lincoln has also passed it on as well.

In the meantime, the news has broken about the millions stolen and Reader is back for a cut. Perkins and Collins don't want to give him any as he wasn't there the second night. On 1st May the three of them meet at the Castle pub and are filmed by the police as they come to a compromise and then the film is examined by a police lip reader and the name Carl comes up. This is Carl Wood, known to the police and a past accomplice of Terry Perkins. It's all coming together slowly. The police have bugged Perkins and Collins cars and hear that the major and final 'divi' is to take place on the 19th May at Perkin's daughter's house as she is away on holiday. The police wait until the divi is underway and swoop on all the houses and offices associated with the gang members. 100 officers are involved. All the suspects are arrested but of 'Basil', there is no sign. He had taken his divi on the Saturday night before they left the Depository and was the man brought in to disable the alarms by Reader. He was not known to the rest of the gang.

Only one third of the total believed stolen was recovered. Reader, Perkins, Jones, Collins and Wood were tried and sentenced. A month after the trial a review of the CCTV and surveillance material was instigated to try and find 'Basil'. It was noted that surveillance teams had watched Collins meet an unknown man on the 17th April and again on the 24th. They had followed this man and taken film and still images of him but who was he? He lived in a nondescript flat, well

171

positioned for a fast exit by three routes out of the building and he lived 'off the grid'. No utility bills and so no record of who he was. His name was Michael Seed. He was known to the police but not for anything major and had been quiet for a number of years. The police watched him for two years after the robbery waiting for a mistake. One wasn't forthcoming but profilers noted that Seed had a particular way of walking that swung his right leg in front of his left at an angle. This tied up with the grainy image of the man with the bag on his shoulder at the depository who had the key. A warrant was issued and Seed's flat raided on the 17th March 2018. Inside was a gold smelter, gold, gems and £150,000 of banknotes. He got ten years.

THE ROBBERY as newspaper and personal reports

April 2015, the Hatton Garden Safe Deposit Company, an underground safe deposit facility in London's Hatton Garden area, was burgled. The total stolen may have a value of up to £200 million, and the incident has been called the 'largest burglary in English legal history.'

The heist was planned and carried out by four elderly men who were experienced thieves, all of whom have pleaded guilty. Four other men are being tried on suspicion of involvement. The burglary occurred during a period in which both the Easter Bank Holiday and Passover coincided. Being in the Jewish area of Hatton Garden this may well have been taken into consideration with the date planning. The police first announced it had taken place on 7th April although the crime was started on 2nd April. Were the police keeping quiet whilst they tried to find the gang and spoke to their 'grasses' about it? Why such a period of silence? The Met won't comment. There was no external visible sign of forced entry to the premises. Somebody had a key or was a very good lock picker. Once inside the gang abseiled down a lift shaft, drilled through 50cm concrete wall with a Hilti DD350 drill (£3,000) first off they hit a steel safe back and had to fetch a more powerful drill and in then a wrench that pushed through. Then once in they helped themselves to the contents of 70 safe boxes. On 8th April, press reports emerged speculating that a major underground fire in nearby Kingsway may have been started to create a diversion as part of the Hatton Garden burglary. The London Fire Brigade later stated that the fire had been caused by an electrical fault, with no sign of arson. A CCTV recording of the incident was released by the Daily Mirror before the police released it. The video recording showed people nicknamed by the newspaper as 'Mr Ginger, Mr Strong, Mr Montana, The Gent, The Tall Man and The Old Man'.

On 22nd April, the police released pictures of the inside of the vault showing damage caused by the burglary, and how the burglars had used holes drilled through the vault's wall to bypass the main vault door.

On 19 May, the Metropolitan Police announced that nine arrests had been made in connection with their investigation into the raid. On 1st September 2015, it was announced that the Hatton Garden Safe Deposit Company had gone into liquidation as the business had become insolvent because 'trade dried up' as a result of the robbery.

Timeline

On 1 April 2015, electrical cables under the pavement in Kingsway caught fire, leading to serious disruption in central London. The fire continued for the next two days, with flames shooting out of a manhole cover from a burst gas main, before being extinguished.

Several thousand people were evacuated from nearby offices, and several theatres cancelled performances. There was also substantial disruption to telecoms infrastructure. On 8th April, press reports emerged stating that the fire may have been started as part of a distraction plan for the burglary.

2nd   April: late afternoon Hatton Garden Safe Depository staff lock the doors and leave for Easter weekend

2nd   April: 21:23 'Mr Ginger' descends to the vault, followed by three men pulling wheelie bins

2nd April: 00:21 police at Scotland Yard are informed that the burglar alarm has been triggered but do not attend.

3rd   April: 08:05 gang members talk before going to their van and driving away

3rd April: 21:17 'Mr Ginger' goes down into vault, and is later joined by two other men

3rd   April: 06:10 the gang members drive away from the building

7th   April: Scotland Yard state they are aware of the burglary

10th April: The Daily Mirror releases CCTV footage

19th May: The Metropolitan Police announce that they have arrested nine suspects

Arrests

On 19 May 2015, 76-year-old Brian Reader, who was involved in laundering the proceeds of the Brink's-Mat robbery, and his 50-year-old son Brian were arrested in connection with the robbery by flying squad officers. In November 2015, Carl Wood, William Lincoln, Jon Harbinson and Hugh Doyle were all arrested and charged with conspiracy to commit burglary and conspiracy to conceal, convert or transfer criminal property.

Jon Harbinson - Lincoln's nephew - was cleared of playing a part in the heist and set free after eight months in custody. Four men - Brian Reader, Kenny Collins, Terry Perkins and Daniel Jones admitted conspiracy to commit burglary. Another man, known only as "Basil", who let his co-conspirators into the Hatton Garden building by opening the fire escape from inside is yet to be identified. The police are offering a £20,000 reward for information leading to his arrest and conviction.

Reviewing lawyer Ed Hall from the Crown Prosecution Service said: 'The four main ringleaders, a close-knit group of experienced criminals, some of whom had been involved in other high-value crimes, pleaded guilty after realizing the strength of the case against them. As a result of this trial, three other men who played significant roles, including the moving and concealing the stolen gold and jewels, have also been convicted.'

Perkins' daughter, Terri Robinson, 35, of Sterling Road, Enfield, pleaded guilty to concealing, converting or transferring criminal property. Her brother-in-law, Brenn Walters, 43, who is also known as Ben Perkins, admitted the same offence. Both received suspended sentences.

The Met Police had faced criticism over its handling of the case after it emerged it had not followed procedures after receiving a call from a security firm about an intruder alert at the premises at midnight on Good Friday.

Following the verdict, Det Supt Turner said: 'We apologise for not actually attending the alarm. It is quite clear that police should have attended. We have reviewed all our systems and processes.'

The Hatton Garden burglary was unquestionably audacious. It was a crime that required cunning, strength and physical fitness. The gang responsible switched off most of the alarms and security cameras. They clambered down a lift shaft to get to the vault. They spent hours drilling through concrete. They forced open 73 safety deposit boxes.But this wasn't the work of a gang of young, ambitious criminals it was the work of a group of men in their 60s and 70s who came from the old school where plots were formed over a pint in a pub on a Friday night.

So why on earth would they bother with such a complicated crime at their age? Why would they take such a risk at a time when most people of their age would be contemplating or enjoying their retirement, the Hatton Garden gang had other ideas. Forget gardening and cruises they spent around three years plotting the daring raid.

'You can almost picture the joy and excitement that planning would bring,' says David Wilson, professor of criminology at Birmingham City University. 'I imagine the more they spoke about it, the more excited they became. This was the one last dream job. There is a great deal of excitement in committing this kind of crime. There is a great deal of status attached to it.' Brian Reader, Terry Perkins, John (Kenny) Collins and Danny Jones have a combined age of 278.

They all have a criminal record of varying degrees of severity and that is significant in understanding why they found the Hatton Garden plot just impossible to resist.

Brian Reader, known as The Master, 76, Danny Jones, 60, John (Kenny) Collins, 75, Terry Perkins, 67, William Lincoln, aka Billy the Fish, 60, Hugh Doyle, 48, Carl Wood, 58, Michael Seed, "Basil", unknown. 'The fact that they're in their 60s and 70s shouldn't surprise us because they've previously engaged in criminal enterprise,' says Prof Wilson. 'This kind of enterprise gives them excitement, makes them feel alive and takes them out of the banality of their everyday lives.'

Most of these men were on many levels your typical group of pensioners. Brian Reader used a free bus pass. Kenny Collins was the lookout who frustrated others in the gang who said he fell asleep during the raid. Terry Perkins was a diabetic who took all his medication into the vault with him in case he needed it.

Perkins had also been jailed before for his involvement in another notorious crime back in the 1980s. He was given a sentence of 22 years for his part in the raid on the Security Express Headquarters in east London in 1983. (see that section in the book)

Also jailed for his role in the Security Express raid was Freddie Foreman. He is now approaching 94 and is reflective about his criminal past but totally understands why the Hatton Garden gang thought they could get away with the burglary.

'If they'd asked me to join them I might have found it hard to say no,' he says. 'Even though my legs aren't what they used to be, it's the excitement, the respect you get and it's the thought of doing one last big job.'

And that seems to be fundamental to this particular crime - the idea of one last thrill. Even at their age they just couldn't resist it. But their final crime was too ambitious and they were perhaps a bit naive. They underestimated how CCTV and surveillance would ultimately help the police track them down.

Who's who in the Hatton Garden heist gang and how much do they have to repay?

Brian Reader was known as 'the Guv'nor' and was a partner in crime of notorious gangland figure Kenneth Noye - the pair were like 'chalk and cheese'.

Aged 76 at the time of the robbery, Reader is the oldest of the gang and he even travelled to the robbery on a bus using a pensioner's 'Freedom Pass'. One police officer even described him as 'the last of the gentlemen thieves.' Under the proceeds of crime act he was told he must pay back

£6,644,951, including the sale of his £639,800 home and development land worth £533,000.

Daniel Jones, 58 at the time, was described as an 'eccentric Walter Mitty' character during the trial when one of the accused men told of his strange habits. He is one of the two men who actually got through the small hole the gang drilled into the vault and went through safety deposit boxes before handing the loot back through the hole to the others to sort.

He was caught on CCTV wearing an eccentric outfit during the raid, complete with striped trousers, a hi-viz waistcoat, red trainers and a navy baseball cap. He was ordered to hand over £6,649,827 under the proceeds of crime act.

John 'Kenny' Collins, 75 at the time, was part of the Islington side of the gang and has a long string of convictions for crimes including robbery, handling stolen goods and fraud dating back to 1961. He was the driver for the gang who waited in vehicles outside the safety deposit company on both nights of the Hatton Garden raid and acted as a lookout from a rented office opposite. It was his link to the white Mercedes which was the first step in police tracking down the raiders. He was ordered to pay £7,686,039 under the proceeds of crime act after the court heard he had assets in 'liquid form' and property in this jurisdiction and abroad.

William 'Billy' Lincoln, 60, was recruited by ringleader John 'Kenny' Collins as a trusted family member to control a large part of the loot following the heist. He has a string of convictions for attempted burglary, burglary and attempted theft between 1975 and 1985, but his most recent conviction was for battery in 2013. The married father-of-two was a well known character at the famous Billingsgate fish market where he would buy haddock, kippers, eels and salmon to sell on to friends and family members. He was consequently known as 'Billy the fish' . Lincoln was ordered to pay a much smaller £26,898 under the proceeds of crime act for his lesser role in the plot or face another nine months in jail.

Terry Perkins was one of the key players behind the Hatton Garden burglary, Perkins, of Enfield, was told he must pay £6,526,571 under the act. He died in prison shortly afterwards. Exactly 32 years earlier, on April 4 1983, he celebrated his 35th birthday by carrying out an armed robbery on the headquarters of Security Express, on Curtain Road, in Shoreditch.(see earlier in the book) He was part of a gang of masked robbers who made off with £6m in what, at the time, was Britain's biggest cash robbery. Perkins was jailed for 22 years at the Old Bailey in 1985, along with John Knight, where they were described as 'two evil, ruthless men'. Carl Wood, 58, was a trusted associate of the ringleaders, recruited as an 'extra pair of hands' to pull off the heist. Wood grew up in Hackney, has been married to wife Paula for 19 years and has two adult daughters who have children of their own. He was diagnosed with Crohn's disease in his early 20s, an inflammatory bowel disease which he claimed often left him bed-ridden and in agony. Wood, 60, of Cheshunt, Hertfordshire, has been ordered to pay back £50,000 under the proceeds of crime act.

Hugh Doyle, 48, was a plumber and trusted friend of John 'Kenny' Collins who offered up his yard as an exchange point for the handover of stolen goods between vehicles. He had no part in the raid and made no financial benefit from it. He was fines £367.50 for his 'general criminal conduct'. One benefit for Doyle was that a long lost son recognised a likeness to old photos and got in touch.

After the Hatton Garden heist an allegation has emerged that the whole thing was financed by 'a London gang'... the only gang capable of the finance is probably the Adams family who had warned the Hatton Team off a few years earlier when they had originally sought finance for the robbery. Now they, if it was them, put in their own man on the team to keep an eye on it, that man was 'Basil' the man the rest of the team didn't know and who always wore a ginger wig and disguise. He was the man who had the keys to the Hatton Garden building. When the team entered the vault Basil went straight away to one box and took it out of the building with him, unopened. That was all he took although he plundered the jewellery the others had taken at a later meeting a few weeks after. So what was in that one box? Rumour has it that the only way John Palmer could keep alive in the UK when he returned (see Palmer section) was because he had some major evidence on a major gang and their murders and their involvement in the Brinks Mat heist in which Palmer was a major fence. If anything was to happen to him his partner was to hand that evidence to the Police, it is alleged that evidence was in the box in the Hatton Garden Vault that 'Basil' made a bee line for. Draw your own conclusions. One last observation. I ask again, where did the key to the back door of the Depository come from?

****

CHAPTER 27

JACK 'THE HAT' McVITIE

Jack 'the hat' McVitie, was an enforcer, a hit man, a killer, if somebody stepped out of line 'call in Jack'. He was known as 'the hat' because he always wore a trilby. Many said this was because he was prematurely bald and wanted to conceal it. Frankie Fraser, another 'enforcer, spent time in his company in prison and became friends with the man he called 'lovely'. Two peas in a pod eh? But in the mid 60s he expanded from debt collecting and contract killing and became embroiled in the drug scene becoming an addict himself which led to a falling out with the Kray twins for whom he had 'done some work' before. The result of the drug taking was that he was getting abusive to others and very arrogant. He got thrown out of Freddie Foreman's night club in Balham for causing trouble and pretty soon was not welcome in most others. He even tried to shoot Tommy Flanagan in the Regency Club and had a knife fight there in the basement which had him thrown out only to return and threaten the owners John Barry and his brother. The Barrys had a quiet word with their club 'protectors' the Krays and asked them to sort McVitie out before he ruined theirs and others clubs businesses.

The Krays did have a quiet word, more than once, but McVitie didn't listen and although not a member of 'the firm' he had done jobs for them and owed them money for not fulfilling one contract which was the murder of their business manager Leslie Payne who they thought was about to tell the police about their criminal activities. McVitie got paid £500 upfront for it but in the end took so long they had somebody else do it and wanted their money back. Reggie Kray had one last meeting with Jack and although he gave him a severe warning about his behaviour he came away from the meet convinced that Jack wouldn't alter and would become a bigger embarrassment unless stopped. A plan was hatched to kill McVitie.

The following evening 29th October 1967 Tony and Chris Lambrianou had a night out at the Carpenters Arms where the Krays were holding court. Tony was a member of The Firm, Chris wasn't and they worked the Birmingham area. After a few drinks the Lambianous moved onto the Regency club where they were joined by Jack McVitie, Johnny Hart and the Mills brothers Tony Lambrianou left them for a while and returned with the news that they were invited to a party at 'Blonde' Carol's Basement place at Evering Road, Stoke Newington where plenty of women were available. It was a set up, Tony had left not to go Blonde Carol's but to meet Reggie Kray upstairs at the Regency where he had been told to get McVitie down to Blonde Carol's at Evering Road. When they got there the Krays were there with two minders, Firm members Ronnie Bender and Ronnie Hart and the Mills brothers. Reggie gave McVitie a real tongue lashing and true to form McVitie gave one back. Reggie held a gun to McVities head and pulled the trigger, twice, and both times nothing happened. Reggie Kray then killed him with a knife.

The Mills brothers scarpered quickly knowing what was going to happen, Chris Lambrianou also left getting a hostess called Connie Whitehead to drive him home. Then at home he had a change of heart and worried about his brother Tony so he armed himself and went back. His brother Tony was safe outside but in the basement he found Jack McVitie dead and Ronnie Bender who had been left to clean it up and dispose of the body wondering what to do.

Tony Lambrianou tells a different story, he says that when the gun wouldn't fire Reggie told Chris to go and get another one. McVitie put up a fight but Reggie Kray used a knife to stab him in the chest and face until he was dead in a ferocious attack. The twins then quickly left leaving the others to clean up and do the disposal. The body was wrapped in an eiderdown and put in the back of Tony Lambrianou's car with brother Chris and Reggie Bender following in another car. The plan was to dump it in South London so the Richardson's would get the blame. But they panicked and dumped it just on the south side of Rotherhithe Tunnel outside St Mary's Church, Rotherhithe. When the Krays were told they went mad as this was Freddie Foreman's patch and they were great friends. A call was made to Freddie who had the body picked up and moved before anybody else found it. Where did it end up? Only Freddie Foreman knows and he's in his 90's now in a care home and probably will take the secret to the grave. Some say it went to a pig farm in Essex, some say it went out to sea at Newhaven and was dumped with weights attached and some say it's in a grave at Gravesend Cemetery, Kent.

(as a side to this, old gang wars never die…at Thomas Wisbey's (Grt Train Robber) funeral in February 2017, Foreman then 82 and Eddie Richardson then 84 had a punch up in the pews….true.)

****

CHAPTER 28

1940s – 1990s FREDDIE FOREMAN

Freddie Foreman is a career criminal associated with a number of major heists. He was active 1940s-90s first arrested on an assault charge in 1948 when he was a member of the shoplifting gang known as the 40 Thieves. His first major conviction was in 1952 when he got 9 months for armed robbery and was sent to Wandsworth prison. Over the next few years he built his own criminal organisation whose members included Buster Edwards and Tommy Wisbey (Grt Train Robbers) and Billy Hart. They made several robberies all over London until an 'off patch' Southampton armed robbery went wrong in 1960 and he got 3 months in Wandsworth. After his release his escapades came to the notice of the Kray twins during their battles with the Richardsons and he helped them when needed, including killing for them and as a reward had their protection. In that period he gathered a new gang around him and established a turf in the Deptford area of London. They robbed banks, post offices, security vans, company payrolls and other walk in armed robberies which was their signature crime. A robbery of a payroll delivery van in Bow in 1961 nearly had them all caught as armed police officers were waiting but they managed to get away.

Their main success was a gold bullion van robbery in Stepney in 1961 with various amounts up to £2m stolen were bandied about. With his gang members Wisbey and Edwards plotting the Great Train Robbery with Gordon Goody and Bruce Reynolds, Forman was asked to join them but turned the offer down. But in 1965 he did provide a safe house for escaped Train Robber Ronnie Biggs and in 1966 arranged the deal that saw Buster Edwards give himself in for a reduced sentence. It is alleged he was also involved in getting Charlie Wilson out of Winson Green. Wilson got as far as his villa in Spain where he was shot dead two years later.

Frankie Fraser claimed that Foreman was the instigator of the killing of Ginger Marks after Marks and Jimmy Evans had shot Freddie's brother George Foreman who was having an affair with Marks wife. Evans testified against Foreman for the murder of Marks in 1975 but Foreman was acquitted, although later in his book he admitted he and Alfie Gerrard had murdered Marks. Had Foreman been a younger man at the time of his admittance the police may well have retried him as the law of Double Jeopardy had been abolished between the acquittal trial and his admitting the crime. In his dealing with the Krays, Foreman shot and killed Frank Mitchell on their orders and as a personal thank you to the twins for their protection. Jack McVitie half wrecked Foreman's night club in Balham in a drunken fight in 1967, the club was under the protection of the Krays and McVitie had made loud threats to Foreman and the Krays as he was thrown out. (see Krays and McVitie sections). After the Krays killed McVitie the body was dumped on Foreman's manor and he disposed of it. He was later convicted of involvement in McVitie's killing and sentenced to ten years in 1969. Foreman acquired the nickname 'Brown Bread' cockney rhyming slang for 'dead' after these murders.

He fled to the USA in 1979 after his connection to a drugs raid in which a customs official had been killed was discovered. He was arrested in 1981 when he came back to the UK after brokering a two year suspended sentence for the raid. The major Security Express raid was allegedly his plan and he fled to Spain which had no extradition laws with the UK and lived in a magnificent villa in Marbella for several years alongside many other UK criminals. The law changed and he was extradited to the UK in 1988 and convicted of laundering the money from the Security Express raid and sentenced to nine years in 1990. I think he is still around at the time of publishing this book and in a care home in London. His son Jamie is a respected actor and a good one at that.

Freddie has 8 books out and his latest one is an autobiography called 'Respect'. Amongst all the 'true' books from criminals of the 60s- 90s my view is that 'Respect' is by far the one that hits the mark, or should I say Marks?

****

CHAPTER 29

1970s-now THE ADAMS FAMILY

'Everybody stood up when he walked in. He looked like a star,' recalls David McKenzie, a London financier talking about Terry Adams. 'He was immaculately dressed in a long black coat and white frilly shirt. He was totally in command.' Indeed, the middle-aged man described by McKenzie as looking like 'a cross between Liberace and Peter Stringfellow' was entitled to have an air of authority he was/is the head of an international business empire worth an estimated £200m. Its employees are, by the very nature of that empire, few in number and unswervingly loyal. The man's home, where McKenzie was introduced to him, is a discreetly guarded but substantial north London mansion, tastefully decorated and filled with antique furniture and expensive objets d'art. He is a well-mannered man of cultured tastes, with a liking for good wine and custom-built cars. He was once so wealthy that he considered putting in a bid for Tottenham Hotspur Football Club. But this is no ordinary captain of industry. His name is Terry Adams and he was, and still is, the head of Britain's most enterprising (and most feared) organised criminal gang, the Adams family, otherwise known as the A-Team, or the Clerkenwell Crime Syndicate. Their 'business' began with petty extortion from market traders, moved into armed robbery and finally blossomed into drug trafficking, all backed up by a willingness that led to their alleged involvement in up to 30 gangland killings. Their ability to evade justice gave them an air of invincibility, fuelling the belief that they had detectives, lawyers and prosecutors on their payroll and that even jurors were not immune from their menaces. Anyone considered an informer against them or a threat to the family was ruthlessly targeted. 'A formidable and feared organisation steeped in the highest levels of criminal activity,' one Old Bailey trial was told. Or, as one gangland expert put it, 'they make the Krays look like clowns'.

So how did this extraordinarily powerful crime organisation begin? The three best-known Adams brothers come from an otherwise law- abiding and respectable working-class Irish Catholic family, in one of the less salubrious parts of Islington, north London. Terry was the eldest of 11 children born to truck driver George Adams and his wife, Florence, but it was his younger brothers, Patrick, otherwise known as Patsy, born in 1955, and Sean, otherwise known as Tommy, born in 1958, with whom he became most closely associated.

As said above, the three brothers began their criminal careers by extorting money from traders and stallholders at street markets close to their home in the Clerkenwell area, before then moving on to armed robberies. Patsy found himself serving seven years in jail in the 1970s for armed robbery offences.

By now, Terry Adams had emerged as the brains of the operation, chairing their meetings in a businesslike fashion, with financial matters dealt with by Tommy, and the 'muscle' supplied by Patsy. It is believed the Adams family name became so notorious that they even rented it out, allowing other gangs to say they were working for them to bolster their criminal reputation. This was an income stream first used by the Krays who had an earlier association with the Adams as crime 'mentors'. The difference between the Krays and the Adams is that the Krays courted celebrity and the Adams hate it, they just go quietly about their business avoiding any publicity.

There was a cost of £250,000 per operation for use of the Adam's name and one condition, pay within one week or else. No one would want to be in the position of crossing the A Team or owing them money.

But in the mid-1980s there was a seismic shift in London's criminal culture, led by the Adams family. As Scotland Yard's Flying Squad became more adapt at tracking down armed robbers, and the amount of cash in transit diminished in favour of electronic money transfers, the so-called 'pavement artists', criminals who robbed at street level, post offices, banks and security vehicles, moved into a new and infinitely more lucrative field, drug trafficking. This was a trade fuelled by the demand for cocaine and cannabis during the 1980s, and ecstasy during the 1990s. And it was a trade hitherto largely, although not exclusively, the preserve of amateurish and often ideologically-motivated dealers of the Howard Marks variety. These small-time amateurs and part-timers now found themselves usurped by ruthless career criminals who were more than willing to use violence at the drop of a hat. The vast profits generated by drug trafficking also required new ways of laundering the money. Criminal gangs like the Adams brothers needed to find themselves corrupt financiers, accountants, lawyers and other professionals to help them 'wash' their cash to a squeaky-clean white and then invest it in property and other legitimate businesses. The Adams family are said to have laundered their money through the jewellery quarter of Hatton Garden where they had their base, they used a diamond merchant by the name of Solly Nahome, washing the money through a restaurant in Smithfield and also a West End nightclub. But as their power grew, so did their arrogance and violence. Patsy Adams began to develop a reputation as one of the most violent figures in the underworld, pioneering the use of high-speed motorcycle hit-men to carry out assassinations. An accountant, Terry Gooderham, said to have crossed the brothers by creaming off £250,000 of drug money, was found dead, alongside his girlfriend, in Epping Forest in 1989, a double hit attributed to the Adams empire. One rival Irish family, the Reillys, attempted to challenge the Adams' dominance of their Islington stronghold. In response, Patsy Adams is said to have gone into a pub controlled by the Reillys and allowed one of his associates to insult a member of the rival family. The Reillys, greatly offended, went away to arm themselves and returned to the pub, only to find an ambush awaiting them. Their BMW was fired on repeatedly by members of the Adams gang. No one was killed, but the incident, with echoes of 1930s Chicago, sent out a message both to the Reillys and anyone else who needed to know, the Adams gang was prepared to go all the way to preserve its territory. And it was a territory that rapidly expanded, breaking the unwritten rule that gangs were allowed unimpeded control over their own manors and stayed off other 'firm's' turf, as the Krays had once held sway over east London and the Richardson gang ruled the tract of London south of the Thames. 'What distinguished the Adams from other London gangs, is that they moved into areas that were way beyond the normal territorial ambitions of gangs. They ended up owning practically a whole west London street of bars, which they need for drug trafficking. And their operations spread to places like Lincolnshire and across to Spain,' said one Detective on their track. And their reputation went before them as they reached the peak of their powers in the 1990s. One insider said, 'They created fear just through their name, and undoubtedly a lot of violence was carried out on their behalf. I heard about a guy who owned a bar in west London and some of their people came in one night and simply demanded the keys. He handed them over and got out fast.' They were also willing to take on some of the older remaining members of the gangland community. In August 1991, 'Mad' Frankie Fraser, once a member of the Richardson gang, was shot in the head and almost killed outside a nightclub in Clerkenwell in an attack attributed to the Adams gang. As the drug trafficking continued, they built up links with Yardie groups and the Colombian cocaine cartels, with Tommy reportedlynegotiating an $80m credit agreement from his Latin American associates. They have been linked to 25 gangland murders, using Afro-Caribbean muscle as additional manpower to murder informants and rival criminals. In addition to developing alleged connections to Metropolitan Police officials, they were also stated to have had a British Conservative MP in their pocket at one point. The family is believed to have connections with various criminal organisations, specifically with South American Drug Cartels.

Throughout the Nineties, they seemed untouchable – immune from the law despite the best efforts of dozens of different inquiries, led by Scotland Yard, HM Customs and Excise and the Inland Revenue. Cases against them or their henchmen, either never got off the ground or somehow collapsed. Rumours about the gang having senior detectives in their pay, and their determination to 'get' jurors were rife. The brothers carried on their business separate from normal society, they had no bank accounts, virtually no tax records and may not even directly own the homes they live in. Then, in the late 1990s, things began to go awry. In 1998, Tommy Adams was convicted of organising an £8m hashish smuggling operation, and was sentenced to seven years' imprisonment. When a judge ordered that he surrender £1m of his profits or face a further five years, his wife turned up twice to the court, carrying £500,000 in cash inside a Tesco bag on each occasion. In the autumn 1998, Solley Nahome, who was effectively their principal financial officer, was shot dead outside his north London mansion – in the same street as Terry Adams' home – it was a classic underworld motorcycle hit of the type often attributed to the Adamses themselves. And Wynter another associate, disappeared suddenly. It was later reported that Nahome and Wynter had died at the orders of another London gangland boss associated with the Brinks Mat heist, who believed they had double-crossed him in a cannabis deal. They truth may never be known. But, from about this time, Patsy Adams began spending more time in his Spanish villa.

Terry Adams must have regretted the light that was trained on his activities by these episodes. He carried on as normal, although he is believed to have made strenuous efforts to move as much of the business as possible into legitimate areas, such as property investment. This was hampered by the family's lack of involvement with any legitimate financial institutions or mechanisms, a problem which is said to have scuppered his plans to buy Tottenham Hotspur, which might have required some financial disclosures. Interesting to note he was proposed and backed by David Sullivan and David Gold the ex pornographers who own West Ham FC, (as an interesting aside in January 2021 Sullivan's much younger partner Emma Benton-Hughes joined the board. She is known for her films Horny Housewives on The Job, Lesbian Student Nurses etc. a necessary past experience that no doubt helps in running a Premier League Club!) By the late 1990s a new means arose to tackle the nation's biggest drug dealers. MI5, no longer focused on investigating Irish terrorism and Communist subversion, was charged with helping tackle the massive drug importation problem. Its officers are said to have bugged Adams' homes and cars and followed him closely over a period of several years whilst working in tandem with both the newly created National Crime Squad and the National Criminal Intelligence Agency, as well as the Inland Revenue. Adams, who was almost certainly aware that he was being followed, is at this point thought to have been forced to invent spurious companies and organisations to account for his wealth, claiming at various points to have been employed as a jewellery designer and a public relations executive.

Eventually, in May 2003, Adams, a man, let us not forget, with a spotless record, was arrested and charged with money laundering, tax evasion and handling stolen goods. His wife, Ruth, was charged with similar offences. While free on a bail of more than £1m, he fought a lengthy game to delay his day in court, sacking his legal team twice, ordering the transcription of thousands of hours of taped conversations made by MI5 and once claiming that his IQ was too low to understand the charges. Adams, 52, found himself in a rather different environment from his north London manor across the Thames, when remanded inside the high-security Belmarsh Prison awaiting sentencing for money laundering. He could receive up to 14 years in prison but was almost certain to be sentenced to less – and with automatic parole and time off for good behaviour would be out in half the time sentenced. While Adams' guilty plea to money laundering (thus avoiding a lengthy trial) was hailed by police and the Crown Prosecution Service as the climax of a long-sought, hard- fought quest for justice, the man himself saw it very differently. 'I think Terry Adams will view this as something of a victory, he will consider that, after all the efforts that the police have made to get him over the years, he has done rather well out of this,' said one senior officer. It is certainly was not the first time that encounters with the judicial process have worked out to the advantage of Terry Adams, and other members of the Adams family and their associates. One of Terry's brothers, Tommy, was cleared in 1985 of involvement with the laundering of the £26m Brinks Mat haul, while Gilbert Wynter (see above), one of the family's "enforcers", was tried in 1994 for the murder of Claude Moseley, a former athlete turned drug dealer, only to be acquitted after the main prosecution witness mysteriously refused to testify. Then there was the case involving the aforementioned Mr McKenzie. A Mayfair-based financier, McKenzie was asked in the late 1990s by the Adams family to launder large amounts of drug money on their behalf. However, his investments failed and around £1.5m was lost. McKenzie was duly invited to Adams' mansion in Mill Hill, north London and left in no doubt that the money had to be recouped within 24 hours. A few days later, when the cash was not forthcoming, McKenzie claimed that he was summoned to another meeting, this time at the Islington home of John Potter, Adams' brother-in-law. Here, an Old Bailey jury was later told, one Christopher McCormack, a close associate of the third brother, Patsy, set about Mr McKenzie. As well as being kicked and beaten, sustaining three broken ribs, he was carved up with a Stanley knife to the point where just fragments of skin were keeping his nose and left ear attached to his face. Two tendons on his left wrist were severed, permanently affecting the use of his hand. When Potter gave evidence during the trial, he accepted that McKenzie had been injured at his home, but maintained that the attacker was a total stranger. He was cleared of committing acts intended to pervert the course of justice. When McCormack gave evidence, he admitted meeting McKenzie three times to recover the debt 'or my old mate Patsy', but claimed that the presence of McKenzie's blood on his jacket must have come from an earlier meeting, when he had broken up a fight between the financier and another man. McCormack was cleared, thanking the jury profusely and offering to buy them a drink 'over the pub'. One male juror apparently winked at McCormack and raised his hand in greeting, an incident that was never explained. While these jury acquittals have to be taken at face value, many police officers involved in the investigations expressed incredulity at the decisions. Belief that the Adams brothers were attempting to interfere directly with the judicial process was confirmed not long afterwards, when Mark Herbert, a clerk with the Crown Prosecution Service, was convicting of selling the Adams family, through an intermediary, the names of 33 informants in return for £500. Adams was subsequently acquitted of charges of importing cannabis worth

£25m as witnesses, named on the informants list, withdrew statements. Admitting that he knew he was signing the informants' death warrants, Mark Herbert said, 'They will send them flowers, but possibly not for their birthdays.' Victor Temple, QC, prosecuting at his trial, told the Old Bailey that this was an organisation that was 'no stranger to the imposition of serious violence against those who might seek to challenge them and few could afford to trifle with their wishes.'

In the end, Adams did what many criminals do., he made a deal, culminating in a brief court appearance, at which he surrendered himself to prison officers. In return for admitting one charge of conspiring to hide £1m, the remaining charges against him and his wife, who has been seriously ill with a stomach complaint, have been allowed to 'lie on the file or, in other words, have been effectively dropped.

Micky Adams sent his 4 children to private schools, had luxury cars and spent his summers in Portugal with his family. He was getting through a minimum £48,000 a year but told HMR he was getting as little as £18,607. He submitted seven false self-assessment tax forms between 2006-2013. He hid money by moving it around and using other people's accounts. His brother Terry, the leader of the family suddenly managed to find £727,000 to pay off the remaining amount on a proceeds of crime order for a million pounds after swearing for years that he was penniless and relied on handouts from friends. However surveillance by HMRC showed him dining at top restaurants, attending the opera and signing up for expensive Spa memberships. Tommy Adams another brother, was jailed for 7 years in 2017 after being convicted of money laundering nearly £250,000 and the last brother Patsy 61, was jailed for 9 years for GBH in 2016 for shooting a former friend in the chest after suspecting him of being an informant.

In 2018 the youngest of the brothers, Micky was been jailed in the last of the Organised Crime Command's prosecutions intended to dismantle the Clerkenwell family. He was sentenced at Croydon Court to 38 months after admitting filing false tax returns after detectives exposed over £560,000 he had hidden from the tax man.

It has been revealed that Terry Adams was the godfather and adviser of playboy businessman James Stunt, recently divorced from Petra Ecclestone, daughter of Formula 1 racing boss Bernie Ecclestone.

Of course, jailing these members of the family still leaves others and 'friends' who no doubt will keep the 'business' running.

The family's downfall came with the assistance of MI5 and the Inland Revenue. MI5, in a unique inter-departmental collaboration the first of its kind after the Cold War ended, played a leading part in the electronic war against organised crime—and turned its sights on Adams's international criminal cartel and with Police and MI5 set up a secret squad to dismantle the Adams organisation, directed from an anonymous Hertfordshire address inside a secret bunker sitting somewhere on the busy Hoddesdon commuter belt into London. Some of the recordings made over a period of 18 months suggested that Adams had retired from front line involvement in crime in 1990.

Police sources believe Adams had an informer and knew he was being monitored and had 'stage managed' many conversations for the benefit of his defence. He, for example, was allegedly caught on tape, in 1998, telling his adviser Solly Nahome that he did not want to be involved with a particular illegal deal, which would affect his legitimate business. The Inland Revenue was suspicious enough to ask Adams to explain how he had amassed his personal fortune including his £2 million house and his collection of valuable antiques. Adams invented a range of unlikely occupations, including jeweller and public relations executive. Transcripts of the surveillance and investigations into several front companies Adams set up proved he was lying.

When he was arrested in April 2003 detectives found art and antiques valued at £500,000, £59,000 in cash and jewellery worth more than £40,000 in his home. On 9 March 2014 at a hearing at the Old Bailey, Andrew Mitchell QC summed up the prosecution's case in saying, 'It is suggested that Terry Adams was one of the country's most feared and revered organised criminals. He comes with a pedigree, as one of a family whose name had a currency all of its own in the underworld. A hallmark of his career was the ability to keep his evidential distance from any of the violence and other crime from which he undoubtedly profited.' On May 18, 2007 Adams was ordered to pay £4.8 million in legal fees to three law firms who had initially represented him under the UK's free legal aid scheme. He was also required to pay £800,000 in prosecution costs.

He admitted a single specimen money-laundering offence on 7 February 2007, and was jailed for seven years; he was released on 24 June 2010, but was recalled to prison in August 2011 for breaching his licence. Also, on 21 May in 2007, he was ordered to file reports of his income for the next ten years. Open case files remain untried on Operation Trinity (see later section) records and rumour still exists that several further prosecutions may eventually come to trial. In May, 2009 media reports suggested that his £1.6 million house was for sale as a result of the fees and costs arising from his 2007 conviction. He was released from prison on June 24, 2010. In August 2011 he appeared before City of London Magistrates court charged with 8 breaches of his Financial Reporting Order imposed upon him in 2007. It is believed he has been recalled to prison for breach of parole.

In July 2014 Adams appeared before a High Court Judge in London where he claimed that he was penniless and living in a one bedroom apartment. Adams was ordered to pay £650,000 under the Proceeds of Crime Act.

Thomas Sean Adams (born in 1958 in London) is allegedly financier for his brothers Terry and Patrick. A married father of four, he still has a home near the family's traditional Islington base, but is now living in Spain. Tommy Adams was charged with involvement in the handling of Brink's-Mat gold bullion but in 1985 was cleared of involvement in the laundering of the proceeds during a high profile Old Bailey trial with co defendant Kenneth Noye. Tommy Adams is suspected of establishing connections to other international criminal organisations including numerous Yardie gangs as well as gaining an

$80 million credit line from Colombian drug cartels. In 1998, Adams was convicted of masterminding a £8 million hashish smuggling operation into Britain for which he was jailed for seven years. At trial he was also ordered to pay an unprecedented £6 million criminal assets embargo, or face an additional five years' imprisonment on top of his seven-year term. On appeal the criminal assets embargo was later reduced by appeal judges to £1m largely due to the CPS not having sufficient material evidence in the form of bank accounts or traceable assets to locate and verify Adams' criminal wealth. Tommy Adams' wife, Androulla, paid his £1m criminal assets embargo in cash just two days before the CPS deadline.

Patrick Daniel John Adams (born 2 February 1956 in London) is regarded as one of the most violent organised crime figures in Great Britain. He gained an early reputation in London's underworld by using high-speed motorcycles in gangland murders and was a suspect in at least 25 organised crime related deaths over a three year period. He was sentenced to seven years in prison in the 1970s for an armed robbery.

Although subordinate to Terry Adams, Patrick sometimes known as Patsy has participated in individual criminal activities. Most notably he is suspected of the 1991 murder attempt on Frankie Fraser; also, according to one account, he assaulted Fraser's son David Fraser with a knife, cutting off part of his ear during a drug deal. During the late 1990s, he was reported to spend much of his time in Spain. The Independent *Newspaper* stated in 2001 that he was 'living in exile in Spain in a walled villa bristling with security cameras a few miles south of Torremolinos'. Patrick Adams and his wife were wanted in connection with an attempted murder in Smithfield meat market in central London on December 22, 2013, and were arrested in Amsterdam on 7 August 2015.

Associates
The 'fixer', Haralambos Antoniades, 48, who was jailed for 63

months for two counts of conspiracy to transfer criminal property and one of conspiracy to conceal criminal property.

Steve Mardon, 58, who runs Camden Cab Company, received the same length of sentence for the same indictments.

Martin Dowd, 49, who planned a series of 'cash runs' from Manchester to pay off his debts to Adams, was also given five-and- a-half years.

Richard Jones, 68, from Macclesfield, was convicted of transferring criminal property. He was handed a two-year prison term, suspended for two years.

FEB 26TH 2014 'OPERATION TRINITY' THE POLICE RAIDS

Hundreds of police officers swooped on addresses across London and the Home Counties in an operation aimed at smashing one of Britain's most notorious crime gangs. Senior members of the Adams syndicate were among 15 people arrested as officers dressed in riot gear descended on 25 properties. Almost £300,000 in cash, designer watches, a handgun, shotguns and other weapons were recovered after years of painstaking investigation.

22 homes were raided serving as bases for an 'established and high profile' criminal gang which the police did not name. It was the Adams. Several business addresses were also raided, including solicitors, accountants and property consultants suspected of laundering money. At one safety deposit box in Central London police officers discovered £25,000 and a stash of expensive watches. In another property, a hidden safe held £100,000. Scotland Yard was desperate to land a decisive blow on the Adams syndicate, which has influence worldwide and has a reputation for extreme violence. It has been connected to at least 25 murders. Police suspect members of drug trafficking, extortion and hijacking but in recent years they have moved into white-collar and high-tech crime, including mortgage fraud.

A specialist police team, codenamed Operation Octopod, has been carrying out surveillance. Detectives believe they have amassed evidence of conspiracy to assault, money laundering, fraud and revenue offences.

The raids were carried out under Proceeds of Crime Act legislation, which investigators hope could help finally smash the gang.

One of the properties raided was the £2.5million Clerkenwell mansion owned by Tommy Adams, and his wife Androulla. Tommy, who once led the syndicate with his brothers Terry and Patrick, was jailed for seven and half years in 1998 after admitting his role in an £8 million cannabis smuggling plot. Neighbours knew him as a 'businessman with a mysterious past'. One said: 'Tommy is a man that no one would ever ask him anything about what he did.'

There is evidence that members of the Adams family have escaped prosecution by infiltrating the police and Crown Prosecution Service. Most of the 200 officers involved in the operation were not told the identities of the targets over fears that the information could be leaked. At one garden flat in Highgate, North London, police seized a 24- year-old man believed to be a key figure in the Adams group. Officers broke through his front door – protected by an iron grille – using a steel battering ram just before 6am. Det Chief Supt Tom Manson, of the Met, said the operation aimed to 'dismantle' the gang. 'This gang has believed they were untouchable but we are determined to prove they are not,' he said.

'The links between this gang and serious and violent crime are well documented, as is their strong influence across London, and, we believe, connections to criminals across Britain and Europe.'

The family crime business, known to many as the 'A Team', was also suspected of links to the Russian mafia and the powerful Columbian cocaine cartels. Solicitors, accountants and investment advisers with links to the notorious gang were ordered to hand over documents under the proceeds of crime act, so they could be examined by financial investigators. Some of the solicitors and financial advisors were also taken in for questioning on suspicion that they helped to run the finances of the gang as mortgage brokers and property developers.

The massive hit against the gang was launched after detectives apparently uncovered evidence of crimes including conspiracy to assault, money laundering, fraud and revenue offences. The money confiscated totalled around £275,000 in cash, collected in safes and safety deposit boxes, in addition to luxury items like Rolexes, and computers and phones, which were used for financial correspondence.

Scotland Yard said at one property they found a safe with

£100,000 'tucked away'. The operation was part of a Scotland Yard case against the gang, which has taken months of detectives following money trails to link the properties with the gang's criminal gains. While Scotland Yard did not name the criminal ring, which is also known as the A Team, they did call it 'one of the UK's longest established and high profile organised crime gangs'.

Detective Chief Superintendent Tom Manson of the MPS Specialist, Organised and Economic Crime Command, said: 'We believe we have arrested members of the most long established and high profile crime gang in London. This was a painstaking investigation and a discreet operation run by specialist officers until today when the combined resources of the Met were deployed on the arrest phase of the operation. The links between this gang and serious and violent crime are well documented as is their strong influence across London, and, we believe, connections to criminals across Britain and Europe. We believe they are responsible for a multi-million pound criminal business laundering the profits from crime and using this money to commit other money-spinning offences. This is cash which can be used to fund further crime and provide luxurious lifestyles. For too long organised gangs have used advances in technology that have allowed them to hide their criminal gains and some even believe they can escape justice by bribing those who enforce the law. This operation and others like it are the Met's response. Any criminal gang operating in London needs to know that we will tackle them head on and hit them where it hurts most, by seizing their cash and assets.'

People arrested during the raids, and their charges:

55 year old man – Islington – Suspicion of money laundering

54 year old female – Islington – Fraud

44 year old man – Waltham Forest – Suspicion of Money Laundering, & conspiracy to assault

50 year old man – Islington – Conspiracy to assault, suspicion of money laundering

55 year old man – Haringey – Conspiracy to assault, suspicion of money laundering

49 year old man – Haringey – Suspicion of Money Laundering, Fraud

51 year old man – Barnet – Suspicion of Money Laundering, Fraud

21 year old man – Waltham Forest – Suspicion of Money Laundering, Fraud

58 year old man – Camden – Suspicion of Money Laundering, Fraud

40 year old man – Kilburn – Suspicion of Money Laundering, Fraud

24 year old man – Camden – Suspicion of Money Laundering, Criminal Damage

56 year old man – Herts – Suspicion of Money Laundering

61 year old man – Kent – Suspicion of Money Laundering

57 year old man – Herts – Money Laundering

All were held at a central London police station while searches continued.

Since 2012, the Metropolitan Police Service has restrained, forfeited and confiscated over £62million in criminal cash and assets under the Proceeds of Crime Act of 2002.

****

CHAPTER 30

1980S – present day. THE HUNT GANG

David Charles Hunt (born April 1961 in Canning Town, London) is an English organised crime boss, linked to violence, fraud, prostitution and money laundering. He heads a gang dubbed The Hunt Syndicate, which has been described as being an extensive criminal empire that has so far evaded significant penetration from law enforcement. Hunt is known in gangland circles as Long Fella due to his height of 6ft 5 inches.

A self-described property tycoon, Hunt has been described by Metropolitan Police sources as being 'too big to bring down'. He became a close friend and associate of Reggie Kray, visiting him in prison in 2000 just prior to his death. He was the owner of 'Hunt's Waste Recycling' in Dagenham, which during the nearby 2012 Olympics closing ceremony, was the centre of the 'largest fire in several years' in London which saw 40 fire engines and over 200 fire fighters attend it. Now known as Connect Waste the recycling centre is run by Hunt's longtime friend, Phil Mitchell.

Hunt resides in a 7 bedroom mansion in Woodside Green, Great Hallingbury on the Essex/Hertfordshire border, close to Bishop's Stortford. Complete with swimming pool, tennis court, gym and guard dog pen, the mansion was purchased in September 1993 for £600,000 whilst Hunt, who was 32 at the time, was claiming to be working as a scaffolder, scrap metal dealer and bouncer. In 2013, it was revealed that Hunt had failed to declare any income or pay tax between 1982 and 1996, and he was unable to recall in court how he had been able to afford the property.

Hunt was born in 1961 in Canning Town to May (née Wicks) and George Hunt, the youngest of 13 children. In the mid 1980s, Hunt joined The Snipers street gang who were involved in lorry hijackings in Essex and East London. Six members of his family were already members, with police intelligence reports identifying David and his brother Stephen as two of the main leaders. He was arrested 7 times during his time with the gang, but witnesses would drop their allegations. In 1986, he was given a nine- month suspended jail sentence for handling stolen goods and possession of a sawn-off shotgun. He then moved into the Soho sex trade, purchasing property that operated as a pornography shop and brothel. Police intelligence also put him at the centre of a criminal network involved in protection rackets at nightclubs and pubs.

A police investigation into The Hunt Syndicate, codenamed operation Tiberius, concluded that it had managed to evade prosecution through a mixture of utilising corrupt police contacts and the intimidation of witnesses. The gang were uncovered by the crime squad in Newham, East London in 2006, when a scrap yard in the Docklands area of East London was searched for stolen metal. When another nearby property was raided as part of that operation, 42 containers were unexpectedly discovered to contain the contents of 18 lorry thefts and a commercial burglary. Counterfeit goods were also seized. Dave McKelvey, head of the crime squad, discovered that the gang had been corrupting police officers for over a decade and that despite a gang insider leaking information to the police, the information was never acted upon. Despite overwhelming evidence, the case collapsed after a corrupt anti-corruption detective sent a dossier to prosecutors raising concerns about McKelvey, who was then investigated for two years (the investigation was found to be fatally flawed and McKelvey exonerated, with Detective Chief Superintendent Albert Patrick stating that he struggled to understand what McKelvey was being accused of). As a result of the raids, McKelvey was informed whilst interviewing a petty criminal that a known contract killer had been contracted for £1m to kill 3 police officers including McKelvey himself, who now lives under round the clock protection.

In 2004, a book written by former Hunt associate Jimmy Holmes under the pseudonym Horace Silver, titled Judas Pig, was published. Presented as a fictional book based on a career criminal called Billy Abrahams (Holmes), it was in fact a thinly disguised autobiography of Holme's time as a career criminal during the mid- 80s and through to 1995, with the names of well known living gangsters' names changed to avoid libel action. Hunt, referred to in the book as 'Danny' is exposed as a violent gangland boss, who is responsible for numerous murders and serious assaults whilst running drug/porn/protection operations in London and Essex. Danny (David Hunt) falls out with Abrahams (Jimmy Holmes) and puts a contract out on his life. A follow up book titled 'The Charity Committee' was re-written and published in July 2013, with the real names of the main protagonist included. The book is currently difficult to obtain, as it was withdrawn by Amazon due to a complaint from Hunt's solicitors. In 2013, Hunt unsuccessfully tried to sue The Sunday Times, who three years earlier had exposed him as a violent 'underworld king', with the judge stating that it was 'reasonable to describe the claimant as a violent and dangerous criminal and the head of an organised crime group implicated in murder, drug trafficking and fraud'. Hunt was represented by Hugh Tomlinson QC, who is the chairman of the Hacked Off campaign and also a member of the Matrix Chambers group of barristers of whom Cherie Blair is a founding member. Tomlinson portrayed Hunt as a 'rough diamond' who was 'a misunderstood property tycoon whose only passions in life were his family and racing pigeons', and argued that it was not in the public interest for the newspaper to have revealed how Hunt had been embroiled in a gangland turf war over land the Government had been due to buy in the lead-up to the Olympics. During the trial, The Sunday Times employed five professional bodyguards to protect their witnesses. On the second day of the trial the bodyguards walked off the job after being approached in a pub. Another security firm refusing to take the job on due to the dangerous reputation of the Hunt Syndicate. As the article had been based largely on leaked Serious Organised Crime Agency and police documents, the paper had to rely on these as evidence. When the paper approached the Metropolitan Police before publicly disclosing the leaked documents, the Met responded by unsuccessfully trying to sue them for the recovery of those documents and to obtain an order banning their publication. The Met also launched an internal investigation to try and identify the source of the leak. Sunday Times journalist Michael Gillard was named British Journalism Awards Journalist of the Year in 2013 for the expose, but was unable to attend the award ceremony due to security concerns meaning that he was also unable to attend any public events in London.

It was revealed in May 2014 that Lloyds Bank had loaned Hunt up to £5m at the time of the case, after a £4.2 Million loan with Barclays was called in after staff read media reports of the case. It was also revealed that whilst owing The Sunday Times £805,000 in legal costs, Hunt was loaned £1 Million by former pornographer, newspaper owner and current West Ham United F.C. co-chairman David Sullivan. The loan was made from Sullivan's finance firm GC CO NO 102 to Hunt's business Hunt's (UK) Properties. A member of the Treasury

Select Committee believed that the Financial Conduct Authority should investigate the loans.

Contract on Metropolitan Police Officers

In 2016 details of a plot to assassinate three police officers who were investigating Hunt were revealed in full detail in an episode of BBC's Panorama. For a £1million contract, Hunt had summoned Yardie hitman Carl 'The Dread' Robinson to a boat in Marbella and instructed him to kill the officers. Despite the detectives being tipped off there was a contract against them their superiors, instead of investigating this, suspended the three officers and investigated them for corruption. They were later cleared of any wrongdoing.

Panama Papers

Amidst the Panama Papers leak of April 2016, it was revealed by The Guardian that Hunt was a client of Mossack Fonseca and owned an offshore company, EMM Limited, which held ownership of an iron and steel business in East London.

THE END

****

Barry Faulkner is the youngest son in a large extended family of South London petty criminals who operated in London from 1940's to 90s. His mother was a top fashion model in the 60s and was determined her youngest would not follow in the family career path and kept him away from it as far as she could. With the house often full of villains it was a difficult task, especially with Faulkner and his best mate Johnny Russell going to the Richardson's scrap yard every Saturday as kids to clean the 'rollers' and other 'faces' cars for 2/6d a time. The golden rule being 'don't open the boot or glove department.'

Faulkner worked in the advertising industry as a copywriter and got lucky with some material sent to the BBC and had a career as script writer/editor for various TV companies. He now writes true crime and crime fiction full time with his DCS Palmer series aa Amazon Best Seller.

****

OTHER BOOKS BY BARRY FAULKNER

Books in the DCS Palmer and the Serial Murder Squad series.

FUTURE RICHES case 1. Murder in the entertainment business.

THE FELT TIP MURDERS case 2. Murder in the City's financial area.

A KILLER IS CALLING case 3. Murder by a WMD hitched to mobile phones.

POETIC JUSTICE case 4. Murder revenge at an Academy of Dramatic Art.

LOOT case 5. Murder as villains pursue Nazi gold surfacing in the UK.

I'M WITH THE BAND case 6. A major rock band members are being murdered one by one.

BURNING AMBITION case 7. An organised crime boss murders to keep his last big heist.

TAKEAWAY TERROR case 8. Two organised crime gangs murder for the lucrative West End drugs turf.

THE MINISTRY OF MURDER case 9. Murders at the Ministry of Health but why?

THE BODYBUILDER case 10. Murdered bodies with missing limbs are turning up. Where are the limbs?

SUCCESSION case 11. The head of an Organised Crime gang is murdered on the street. Who by? Even his family are suspects.

THE BLACK ROSE case 12. The breeder of the first 'black rose' the Holy Grail of plant breeders is murdered. Competition to breed it had been intense but which of those involved stooped to murder?

****

TURKISH DELIGHT Book 1 in the Ben Nevis & The Gold Digger series. Private Eye Ben Nevis gets involved tracking illegal missiles on their way to Iran for MI5 and takes on the Arms Dealers. Explosive!!

NATIONAL TREASURE Book 2 in the Ben Nevis & The Gold Digger series. The daughter of a national treasure actress is missing. Is she being held by Romanian gangsters against an unpaid drug fee? Nevis gets involved and the twists and turns mount up, as do the bodies!

****

Keep up with Barry Faulkner's new books plus 'freebies' here....

www.barry-faulkner.com

Printed in Great Britain
by Amazon

50322330R00118